PUEBLA:
A CHURCH BEING BORN

Gary MacEoin
Nivita Riley

PAULIST PRESS
New York / Ramsey

Library of Congress
Catalog Card Number: 79-91894

ISBN: 0-8091-2279-0

Published by Paulist Press
Editorial Office: 1865 Broadway, New York, N.Y. 10023
Business Office: 545 Island Road, Ramsey, N.J. 07446

Printed and bound in the
United States of America

CONTENTS

*To all who struggle and hope
for the total liberation in
Jesus the Christ that is the
goal of the church being born
of the people in Latin America's
comunidades de base.*

1. Latin America Seeks Liberation

Puebla de los Angeles is a sleepy city of half a million people nestling at an elevation of three thousand feet in a fold of the mountain range that skirts the Pacific Ocean from Tierra del Fuego all the way north to the Arctic Circle. A modern highway running north some sixty miles to Mexico City has done little to change its character. Indeed, it could have been the location of Gabriel García Márquez's gloomy novel, *A Hundred Years of Solitude*. A handful of *caciques* (bosses) tied by blood, tradition, and common interests, control business, politics, commerce, labor, the communications media, and everything else. Supported by a traditionalist church in their commitment to keep their territory free of what they call godless communism, a term that includes the mildest efforts to secure the basic human rights of the majority of the inhabitants, they constitute one of the most reactionary communities in all of Latin America.

Few people had ever heard of Puebla of the Angels until the middle of 1978. Then the announcement that it was to be the site of the upcoming Third Conference of Latin American Bishops turned it overnight into a household word. The processes by which it was chosen are known only to some church bureaucrats in Latin America and Rome. The reasons for the choice gradually revealed themselves. Isolated behind the 9-foot-high walls of the seminary, the bishops would be surrounded exclusively by ultraconservative influences. The local press would constantly warn them that communists had dan-

1

gerously infiltrated the church so that not even all bishops could be trusted. The only demonstration a bishop who ventured forth was likely to see would be of neofascists shouting slogans that called for return of tradition, law and order. Here was nothing to remind them of the anguish, the fear, the suffering, the hunger, the hopelessness that dominate the lives of most Latin Americans.

The choice of such a location already gives a hint of the importance attached by church decision-makers to the upcoming Third Conference. Actually, the world was waiting for it. It was going to be faced with a series of issues of critical concern for the direction and vitality of the church in Latin America. Its decisions would have impact far beyond the realm of religion as normally conceived. They would be supportive of or threatening to the military dictatorships, open or disguised, that control nearly every country in the hemisphere. They would be of concern to the United States and to the Soviet Union because of the potential impact on the geopolitical balance of power of a decision to support the status quo or a decision to commit themselves to the struggle for social change. The global corporations, whose massive profits are decapitalizing Latin America at a more rapid rate than any of the previous exploiters of the colonial and neocolonial centuries, also had a stake in Puebla.[1] A church stand for radical social change would affect them too. Even Europe's politicians were watching anxiously. If Puebla were to follow the lead of major liberation theologians in their criticisms of liberal capitalism, the strong parties of the Left in several West European countries would benefit. It might spell the end of the 30-year domination of Italian politics by the Christian Democrats and bring to power a coalition of socialists and communists.

When it became known that the recently elected pope from Poland, John Paul II, would attend, the tension and anticipation rose. The fact of the pope's visit was itself enough to focus a more intense spotlight of world opinion on Puebla. The

2

many statements he had made since becoming pope had provided little information about where he stood on issues agitating church and state worldwide. But in Latin America, everyone believed, he would be forced to show his hand.

The progressives were pleased with this new development. Total coverage by the electronic and printed media was assured, and that meant that the efforts to make the event something less than an ecclesial meeting, a meeting of some bishops isolated from their own priests and people and from the universal church, would not succeed.

Progressives also stressed the similarities of the Christian community he was to visit with those of his homeland. In both Poland and Mexico, over 90 percent of the people are baptized Roman Catholics, and all of them fiercely identify their religious with their national culture. Both have survived for long and bloody years the efforts of professedly anticlerical regimes to destroy them. The experience has given both of them a sense of the essence of Christianity, a realization that it is not in power or in alliance with brute power that Jesus lives and identifies his own. In this context it would seem logical to expect that John Paul would encourage other Latin American hierarchies to continue and accelerate their withdrawal from the traditional alliance with reactionary governments.

It was further surmised that the pope would contrast the living conditions of Poland with those he would see on his visit. He had grown up in a country that had been leveled to the ground and raped by Russians and Germans acting in unison. Yet Poland, in spite of externally imposed limitations, had since made remarkable progress in providing human living conditions for all citizens. Surely he would have to question the systemic causes for Latin America's failure to make similar progress. He had given a hint of where he stood in an address to the Vatican's Justice and Peace Commission shortly after he was elected pope: "Christians must take the lead in developing ways of thinking and life styles that break decisively with the

3

madness of the consumer society, a destructive and joyless society."

The conservatives, meanwhile, were placing the papal visit in a different perspective. They relied on the fact that John Paul came from a very traditional church, one that had implemented Vatican II very cautiously in order to avoid the internal conflicts that the regime was always quick to exploit. They were quite confident that he would shy away from such theological novelties as Liberation Theology, that he would stress the hierarchical structure and the objective reality and unchangeability of the truths entrusted by Jesus Christ to the apostles and their successors. Others might speak of Christianity as a way of life, but for him it was much more. He was clearly in the line of the heroic defenders of the faith for whom the primary issue was to guard the sacred deposit of revelation and protect the simple faithful from error and deception.

Meanwhile, within Latin America itself, powerful influences challenged the church, pulling and pushing it in diverse directions. In particular, the countless numbers of the hitherto voiceless and invisible were finding voice, self-identification, and leadership in their *comunidades de base* (grassroots communities). They were protesting with mounting stridency the constantly deepening poverty, misery, and oppression of the overwhelming majority of Latin Americans. They were denouncing the institutionalized injustice, the society "in a state of mortal sin," as a French observer had called it some years back. They were begging the bishops to find ways at Puebla to put teeth into their assertion at Medellin ten years earlier. There they had identified the neocolonialism of the national oligarchies and the external neocolonialism of "the international monopolies and the international imperialism of money" as the basic cause of the institutionalized violence under which the hemisphere groaned.

The vast majority of Latin Americans have lived in poverty and powerlessness ever since the Conquest. This phenomenon has been one of the constants of the hemisphere's history. What is new in the recent past is that this state of poverty has existed alongside a significant economic growth, an increase in the production of goods and services at a faster rate than population growth. But the unequal distribution of the economic output has had three negative results. The small oligarchical ruling class is growing richer. Profits exported from the hemisphere to the rich countries have caused and continue to cause a decapitalization of the region of greater proportions than ever before occurred. And the vast majority of the people, some half of them experiencing open or disguised unemployment and the others earning at best a starvation wage, have each year less food, clothing, shelter, and access to education and health facilities than the year before.

Scientific studies have established that this deterioration will continue for many years to come, unless a radical change is effected in socioeconomic structures. Data provided by the World Bank, agencies of the United Nations, and similar independent research organizations say that at least 40 percent of the population of Latin America, some 150 million persons, live below the poverty level, and half of these under conditions that are subhuman. They also show that the wealth is concentrated in the top 5 percent of the population, while the deterioration of living conditions is most rapid among the bottom 20 percent.

The "trickle-down" theory, which holds that by improving the situation of the well-to-do some of the benefits will spill over to the needy, has been proven altogether fallacious both in Latin America and elsewhere in the Third World of poverty. We are forced to recognize not only that there are rich people and poor people, but that the dynamics of the system widens constantly the gap between these two groups, making one group progressively richer and the other progressively poorer.

The approximate causes of the situation thus described are to be found in the kind of industrialization that began in the second quarter of this century and grew rapidly after World War II. The process was geared to produce luxury and semi-luxury goods for the rich and the middle sectors because greater profits were possible from serving these categories than from providing for the elementary needs of the poor. Factory wages, although extremely low, were more attractive than those in the countryside, drawing to the cities potential workers far in excess of the needs and starting the mushrooming of slums that today are a feature of every Latin American city except those of Cuba.

Living conditions had become so bad by the 1960s as to warrant the condemnations of the bishops at Medellin, as just noted. But the following decade brought even worse problems. A world recession that started in 1967, and that is today probably nearing its peak, began to make its impact felt everywhere by the early 1970s. It increased the problems of the "international monopolies" and their oligarchical allies, already having difficulty in accelerating capital accumulation to match the demands of rapidly changing technology. Their solution was to cut the living standards of the poor, so that today the real income of the masses is about half what it was fifteen years ago. A study sponsored by Cardinal Evaristo Arns shows that in São Paulo, the state that has benefitted most from the "Brazilian economic miracle," a minimum-wage earner would have to work 15 hours and 55 minutes a day, 30 days a month, to cover basic expenditures for food, clothing, housing, transport, and similar necessities.[2]

The savage cut in already low living standards could be carried through only with a balancing increase in repression to silence the protests of the victims. Here is the explanation for the proliferation of military dictatorships and the almost total abolition of the rule of law even in countries, like Colombia, with nominally constitutional and civilian governments. In order to maintain order without justice, torture has been institutionalized and "respectablized." Trade unions, student associations and other civic groups have been destroyed or domesticated. The result is a proletarianization of the entire hemisphere.

It is understandable that people should turn to the church as the one surviving institution capable of challenging this "state of mortal sin." But it was not easy for the church to respond. The unjust social and political structures were rooted deep in Latin America. The forms we have seen them take in the second half of the twentieth century are the logical development of a system that began with the so-called Discovery (Conquest) of America. From the first days of the Spanish and Portuguese domination, courageous churchmen had denounced injustice and cast their lot with the native Americans and the new race of mestizos formed by intermarriage of the European soldiers and the native women. But the church as an institution always remained closely identified with the colonizing powers on whom it depended for its material needs, and who in fact chose its leaders and dictated its policies.[3]

2. A New Way of Being Church

The Second Vatican Council (1962–65) brought the first crack in this centuries-long alliance. A major part of that Council's call to the church to repentance and reform centered on its widespread failure to follow the command and example of Jesus to give preferential love and attention to the poor. Latin American bishops began a process of dialogue and reflection with bishops from other parts of the Third World of poverty. As they struggled to find ways to relate with the masses of people in rural and urban slums, people who venerated the institution over which they presided without any clear understanding of its theology or mission, they were helped by a radically new movement that had just begun in Brazil and was spreading to many other parts of Latin America.

This was the *comunidad de base* (grassroots community), a gut response by the oppressed to new sophisticated forms of repression. The military dictatorships had evolved what they called the Doctrine of National Security,[1] a kind of neofascism that used force to destroy or domesticate trade unions, political parties, student organizations, and all other social structures standing between an authoritarian state and the individual citizen, converting the entire population into a proletariat. In self-defense the poor began to form small clusters, usually no more than fifteen or twenty neighboring families, to discuss their problems and attempt to unite their efforts and help each other.[2]

What made the survival of these groups possible was that

they were so small as to be virtually invisible. They developed their internal leadership. Usually, though not always, they had a relationship with a priest or minister; but when they had, it was not the traditional kind in which the clergyman decided and the people performed. The process of their development was greatly influenced by the pedagogic theories of the Brazilian educator, Paulo Freire. Although in exile since the military seized power in Brazil in 1964, he continued to be an influence in Brazil while radiating his ideas elsewhere in Latin America and ultimately in North America and other continents.[3]

Freire's approach became known as conscientização in Portuguese, a word that was quickly adapted into Spanish and English. It is similar to the Socratic method of forcing people to reflect on the reality they are living. It starts by asking them what selected ordinary words mean to them, words such as hungry, poor, barefoot, land, sick. The discussion leader guides the reflection to the point where it becomes obvious to the group that their relationship to the realities expressed by these and similar words is not merely a fact, still less the disposition of a wise providence, but the result of a man-devised system maintained for the benefit of a few. Development of an awareness of a situation of injustice and of a realization that the unjust situation is not inevitable quickly arouses the desire for action for change.

By the time that the Latin American bishops met at Medellin, Colombia, in 1968 for their second general conference, a meeting whose purpose was to update the church in conformity with the decisions of Vatican Council II, the *comunidades de base* had become so vital an element of church life that the final documents recognized the importance of this "new ecclesial reality."[4] Having called for serious theological, sociological and historical study of the phenomenon, the bishops said: "Christians should find the living out of the communion to which they have been called in the *comunidad de base*, that is to say, in the local community that matches the reality

9

of a homogeneous group and which is of such a nature as to allow personal friendly contacts with all the members. The pastoral effort of the church should consequently be directed toward transforming these communities into a 'family of God,' starting with making itself present in them as a ferment that will enable even a small nucleus to become a community of faith, hope and love. The Christian *comunidad de base* is thus the first and fundamental ecclesial nucleus, and it should at its own level assume responsibility for enriching and expanding the faith, and also assume responsibility for the worship that is the expression of faith. It is consequently the first cell of church restructuring and the focus of evangelization, and it is also a primary factor in human advancement."

Medellin saw these grassroots communities as subunits of the traditional parish, to be promoted particularly in rural areas and in city slums. This is in fact where they have flourished, but not in the context in which Medellin sought to place them. At the level of principle, Medellin had been unambiguous. It committed itself to "global, daring, urgent, and basically renewing change,. . . a thirst for complete emancipation, liberation from every subjection, personal growth, and social solidarity." But the bishops were in a tradition of extreme paternalism. Although they sought the liberation of the people, they understood this to mean that they be the liberators. For most of them it was unimaginable that the poor might take the initiative in liberating themselves.

Their vision of the grassroots communities, in consequence, remained a hierarchical one. The parish priest would play the dominant role. Because priests were few, lay leadership would have to be developed, substituting for the priest and controlled by him. Turning to Europe for models, they cast this first leadership in clerical molds, thus encouraging the growth of a new hierarchy, with decision-making from the top down instead of from the bottom up.

Within a short time, however, the grassroots communities

themselves began to change this pattern, and the dynamic movement of today is based on internal leadership. The growth and vitality of this movement has amazed all observers. Recent estimates put the number of grassroots communities in Brazil at 80,000; the rest of Latin America may have as many more. One reason is that the proliferation of military dictatorships committed to destroying trade unions, student organizations, and other civic units that stand between the citizen and the omnipotent state, has left the poor with no alternative way to unite for mutual support. Here, the church umbrella helps, as does the fact that each group is small, usually fifteen to twenty neighboring families, a profile so low as to be almost invisible. Because leadership is internal, there is no central point vulnerable to attack, as happens with hierarchically led bodies.

Another reason, perhaps more important, underlies the growth. The model responds to traditional modes of organization. Effective Roman control of the church in Latin America is as recent as the steamship and other late nineteenth-century improvements in communications. Before that, in Brazil in particular (and today Brazil is the leader in the creation of this "new" way of being church), the typical pattern of church organization was not the parish but the confraternity. The confraternities were democratic. Each elected its directors, and they planned church events, hiring the priest when needed to join with them in celebrating the Eucharist. This concept of organization is still very much alive among the people. It explains much of the popularity of the plethora of sects of Spiritists, Afro-Indian rites, and other syncretisms in Brazil. Every Spiritist center still has its "confraria."

The theology and priorities of the grassroots communities, as distilled in the Liberation Theology that is Latin America's first significant contribution to Christian thought, are radically disturbing equally to the Roman Curia and to dominant politico-economic structures. Gustavo Gutiérrez, a

Peruvian priest working among the poor Indians and mestizos of his country and the recognized leader of the liberation theologians, explains in few words what is distinctive and essential about Liberation Theology.

"Its two basic themes, which were also chronologically the first, are poverty and the approach to theologizing. The first element is the viewpoint of the poor; and for that we have to make a commitment to the poor, to identify with their life, their sufferings, their struggles, their hopes. Theology follows as a reflection that presupposes the earlier act of commitment. The distinction between these two acts is not simply methodological; it is the key idea in a life style, a spirituality."[5]

Because Liberation Theology has been the subject of much discussion in North America and Europe while the grassroots community movement is little known, the Gutiérrez comment deserves to be stressed. The theology is a consequence. The essential prerequisite is the ability of the poor to know themselves as persons, to struggle, to hope. The discovery by the hitherto voiceless millions that they have a voice is the central dynamism in Latin America today.

Leonardo Boff, a leading Brazilian liberation theologian, has described in detail the Third Encounter of Brazil's grassroots communities. The theme of this meeting, held at João Pessõa in July 1978, revealed an organic growth in self-understanding and purpose since a first encounter in 1975 and a second in 1976. The theme of the first was "A Church that Is Being Born of the People through the Spirit of God"; of the second, "Church, a People on the March"; of the third, "A People Liberating Themselves."[6]

João Pessõa assembled 150 participants representing the grassroots movements of all Brazil, together with 17 bishops, 18 pastoral agents, and 9 specialized advisers. This was not (to summarize Boff's evaluation) a reproduction of the traditional church based on a priestly and sacramental axis. It was a new reality "born from the heart of the people themselves by virtue

12

of the innovating Spirit of God, organized by the laity around the word of God and the following of Jesus Christ."

Here the people spoke, Boff stresses, a new fact in the 478 years of Brazil's secular and religious history since the Conquest. Previously, speech was the monopoly of the experts, catechist, priest, bishop, with the people's role limited to hearing and repeating. Now the advisers, pastoral agents, and bishops listened as the people described their suffering, their economic, political, and cultural despoliation, their call for justice, their hunger to participate.

Their talk was concrete, not comforting to the power holders: liberation, cooperation, organization to defend trampled rights, recover stolen land, secure a living wage. The concepts were biblical, in the tradition of Jesus and the other great prophets. But there was little "God" talk. The people do not vivisect liberation and Gospel, natural and supernatural. And they know that they, not the institution, constitute the People of God, the true church of Jesus Christ. As one put it: "The traditional church does not know that it is not the Kingdom, that it is not the community; and it isn't even aware that it does not know this."

We are convinced that the real meaning of Puebla cannot be grasped without listening humbly and reflecting deeply on this voice of hope and commitment rising out of the depths of the abandonment, dehumanization and oppression in which the vast majority of Latin Americans live. We will, accordingly, summarize in a few examples their formulation for the bishops of how they see their reality and what they believe the institutional church can and should do on their behalf.

Here is the essence of the João Pessõa message to Puebla. It is typical of many. "We men and women are rural and factory workers, unemployed slum-dwellers, Indians robbed of our lands. We come from all parts of Brazil, and among us are members of the Evangelical [Protestant] churches. We urge you to bring more light, more courage, more hopes, more certainty of total liberation, so that some will not be laughing while others cry, some fat while others are lean, some overstuffed with food while others starve for lack of land, salary, health, marginalized and without value in the sight of society, although the preferred of God."

On the eve of John Paul's arrival, we had the privilege of participating in a "National Encounter of Mexican Christian Groups for a Church of the People," held at Ajusco, some fifty miles from Mexico City.[7] It was a gathering that departed markedly from the usual meetings of Roman Catholics. The people themselves had planned the "encounter" and they remained in charge of its execution. There was no orderly seating in rows of endless pews set at a lower level and at a discreet distance from robed clerics ranged behind a bedecked altar and flanked by ornate statues under a stained-glass dome. Instead, they stood or sat informally under the dome of heaven, their church a courtyard. All around were humbly constructed buildings where local residents receive medical attention; where children are schooled; and where adults gather in the evening to reclaim their right to literacy—a right denied them as children by the very poverty imposed on them.

Freed from the confines of a building, and from the restrictions of an "up-there" externally imposed leader, these two thousand believers formed a picture of strength—strength born of years of disciplined experience of and reflection on the reality of what it means to be a human person. Having dispelled the ignorance that enabled both church and civil leaders to manipulate them, they no longer believed that their impoverished life was divinely mandated or that God wanted them to wait for the hereafter to savor the pie of justice in the sky. Here were people with a self-identification and group cohesion that left no room for wondering who they were or what they were about.

Not waiting for a priest or bishop to convoke and bless the assembly, one of them took the microphone to announce

14

the "good news," outlining the purpose of the encounter as "an interchange of experience between the grassroots Christian groups and the bishops who are the 'bearers' of the voice of the people in the church of Latin America."

Members of 35 grassroots communities from all over Mexico, plus some from Central America, presented in turn the accomplishments, awareness and needs of their groups. One speaker articulated their hope for the Puebla conference: "That the bishops be as aware as are businessmen and industrialists of the true condition of the *pueblo* (people); and that they support our organizations so that change can be effected peacefully."

A delegate from El Salvador described the atrocities being committed against the people by the military dictatorship. Just four days earlier a priest and four youths had been brutally assassinated, and many people were being "disappeared" by the regime. The report ended with a plea to the bishops, in the name of the church, "to call an end to such inhuman violence."

They waved banners that read: "Don't forget Medellin!"; "Puebla for the *Pueblo*"; "We place our hopes in the bishops at Puebla." They chanted songs that reechoed the call of Moses and of Jesus to abandon the security of slavery and set a course through uncharted deserts to liberation. From the tree tops (literally), from the high walls, from the door-step, from the tightly packed courtyard, their unleashed voices confirmed their unshakable resolve. "*No, no, no basta rezar*" (it isn't enough to pray), they sang. "It takes action to produce results."

The usual "sermon" was replaced by a kind of litany that has its roots deep in antiquity, each proclamation followed by a petition from the throng: "We ask the bishops assembled at Puebla to commit themselves along with the church being born of the people and listen to our voice." For many years, they prayed: "The people suffer from exploitation, injustice,

15

hunger; at times we feel the bishops do not know the poor people through whom Jesus speaks. . . . There are bishops, priests, religious, and lay people who are committed to the people; we hope the bishops will try to understand the new current we constitute in the church, and not crush it. . . . We don't want the church leaders to have the mentality of merchants, making profits by building palaces for the rich while the poor go hungry."

Three bishops who had come to listen and learn gladly accepted the invitation to respond. All three identify themselves as enthusiastically supportive of the direction the grassroots communities are taking, an attitude not shared by many members of the Latin American hierarchy. As we shall see, the official stand of the Puebla Conference was for the type of hierarchically controlled and clerically dominated communities that Medellin had envisaged. First to respond was Bishop Sergio Méndez Arceo of Cuernavaca, a leading spokesman at the Vatican Council, at Medellin, and ever since, for the oppressed in their struggle for justice. For years he has been vilified, misrepresented, and called a "communist" by Mexico's business-dominated newspapers. Just before the bishops were due to meet to elect their representatives to Puebla, the papers published what they said was his Sunday homily but in fact a total travesty. Some conservative bishops accepted the published version as fact and publicly repudiated Méndez Arceo without checking. The desired result was achieved. He was not elected to Puebla.

He now recalled with remarkable objectivity his anguish "when the vultures pounced on me." But, he continued, "I have cast my lot with the poor. I side with the marginated even if we are wrong. I will walk side by side with you; not to point out from above or from a distance what is the road, but seeking together the way, as Jesus did, submerged in the human condition."

Eduardo Proaño, bishop of Riobamba, Ecuador, reaffirming his lifetime commitment to the poor, said: "The church of the poor is the one Jesus established, and this is the church we must bring to life."

Finally, an open letter to John Paul II, signed by those present, was handed to the bishops to deliver. The letter described their poverty and need, thanked the pope for coming, and added: "You come to meet with our bishops. The paper says that they have arranged things so that many of those who truly love us and fight to make our lives a little less harsh will not be among their number. We need this meeting to support us strongly, like that other one [Medellin] that said the people should liberate themselves." They assured John Paul that "you are not bearing the burden alone. . . . We are ready to help you."

Another voice for the voiceless is Elena Martínez, a Guatemalan nun. We met her when we visited the shacks in which several hundred people huddle in an industrial park on the edge of Cuernavaca, also in Mexico. Formerly independent small farmers, they now work in factories because their land was expropriated for industrial use. At least some do, those who have the physical and emotional strength to adjust to the rhythm of industrial production in evil-smelling, health-destroying conditions, with minimal safety devices. Those who work get starvation wages, the others nothing. Yet every effort to organize them to ensure human living levels is bitterly resisted by the employers and the authorities. "They call us communists," Sister Elena told us, "because we are involved in politics. But the kind of politics in which we are involved is the effort to build a juster world. That is not done merely saying rosaries and attending church services."

These grassroots groups, and the many others whose members we met or whose statements we have studied, share a striking quality. Their newfound self-respect and their changed understanding of what is involved in being a Christian include no element of anticlericalism. On the contrary,

17

along with their sense of dignity and group strength they have an almost pathetic hope that the church leaders will accompany them in their struggle to liberate themselves, as Bishop Méndez Arceo committed himself to do. They are not rebels against the church. They want to remain faithful members of a church that is itself faithful to the spirit of its founder.

So far we have sketched in broad outline the reality of Latin America's church and society as seen from one perspective, and we have indicated what should be the concerns of the bishops if they accept this analysis. But others look at the same reality and reach different conclusions about it. Some of these were in a position to exercise major influence on the preparation for and the proceedings of the Puebla Conference. It is time to see who these people were, and why they thought and acted as they did.

3. Can the Church Change?

From the Council of Trent and the Counter-Reformation in the sixteenth century up to the papacy of John XXIII (1958–63), the metaphor Roman Catholic theologians and bishops saw as most aptly describing the church was the Bark of Peter. The pope was the captain on the bridge; the bishops, his officers; priests and nuns the crew; and the faithful, the passengers. It was a stormy sea. Hurricanes were possible at any moment. Pirates could attack without warning. The insidious heresies of the Reformers were everywhere. Even more subtly dangerous was the boring from within of the Modernists who used the new historical and life sciences to challenge the accuracy of the Bible, to question the real intentions of church councils, and to downgrade church laws and practices sanctioned by centuries of tradition.

Most of today's cardinals and bishops were imbued with this siege mentality in their formative years. They entered a minor seminary at an early age, quite often at 10 or 12. From then on they are isolated from the normal influences of human experience and immersed in a homogenized ecclesiastical culture. Their professional studies are either in a Roman university or in a seminary whose professors were trained in Rome. The textbooks were the product of conservative authors of the so-called Roman School, legalistic, casuistic, steeped in the Aristotelian and Scholastic concepts of unchangeable essences, objective truths knowable with absolute certainty, definitions frozen for all time. The student asked no questions, absorbed passively the wisdom handed down to him by his professors.[1]

A long-time member of the Roman Curia and profound admirer of Pope John XXIII has given a devastating evaluation of these universities and educational institutions. "If they are formative at all," Carlos Falconi has written, "they are formative only as regards the intellect, even then only in a distorting sort of way, because their raison d'être is not to promote free scientific research, as in a free university, but to submit the student to a definite ideology under the pretext or illusion that it is identical with the truth."

Additional complicating factors affect the Latin American bishops as a group. The church reached Latin America as a department of the Spanish and Portuguese states charged with specific functions: conversion, education, welfare. The bishops were chosen by the state, a process that still survives extensively, even where formally ended. The church traditionally legitimated whatever regime happened to be in power. With a progressive government, bishops lauded social action. When reactionaries took over, bishops tended to stress law and order or at least stop talking.

The level of education of many churchmen reflects the general level in the Third World. Few do higher studies. Still fewer are familiar with the vast range of physical and social sciences without which a modern society could not function. When a complicated issue arises, they look to those above them to tell them the answer. This inevitably gives enormous leverage to the Roman Curia, on which in addition they depend for preferment and often for subsidies. It also gives enormous power to those cardinals and bishops who are outstandingly educated, forceful, convincing, and political. The stands taken by one such are automatically adopted by the many who accept his leadership.

The 1960s were a period of optimism in church and state. The Vatican Council called and opened by Pope John XXIII

20

raised enormous expectations for a rejuvenation not only of Roman Catholicism but of all Christian churches. Meeting at Medellin in 1968, the Latin American bishops approved a program of profound change that would lead soon to a society worthy of the name of human. It was the decade of the Alliance for Progress under which the United States and the Latin American republics (except Cuba) had committed themselves by treaty to share their resources in a mighty cooperative effort to wipe out poverty in the Americas. Anxious to qualify for large quantities of aid, even the most reactionary regimes were vaunting their rapid progress toward democratic and socially equitable forms. It was easy in all these circumstances to get the bishops to pronounce themselves in favor of radical social change. There were holdouts, as there had been at Vatican II, but everywhere they were a small minority except in Colombia, the one hierarchy that went formally on record as opposed to the Medellin Documents. The consensus in favor was clear.

The early 1970s brought a radical change of attitude in both church and state. A recession started in 1967 and by 1972 was causing concern to governments and people all around the world. The Alliance for Progress and the UN "Decade for Development" had been equally disastrous. Instead of optimistic talk about peaceful social change, governments were building up repressive police and military forces to crush the movements calling for land reform, living wages, and work. For survival, they had decided to maintain the social and economic status quo, even if that meant order without justice.

In the church too, the aftermath of Vatican II was a serious cleavage between those who were frustrated at the slowness of the renewal and at times took the law into their own hands, those who wanted a gradual change thoroughly controlled by the Roman authorities, and those who objected to any change and wanted a return to the legalism and centralism of the pre-Johannine era.

21

The combination of these factors was felt most acutely in Latin America. The Cold War propaganda of the United States had succeeded in convincing the vast majority of civil, military, and religious leaders that the supreme threat to the hemisphere was communist subversion, promoted by outsiders. Were it not for outside agitators, money, and arms, many came to believe, the land invasions by the peasants, the guerrilla movements, and the other evidences of discontent would cease.[2]

By the time of the elections of new officers for CELAM, the secretariat of the Latin American bishops, in 1972, the mood of the church leaders had so changed that they chose as secretary general the extremely conservative auxiliary bishop of Bogotá, Colombia. At age 36, Alfonso López Trujillo had already acquired a reputation as a hard-nosed, hard-driving business executive. He lost no time in getting a firm grip on CELAM's administrative machinery, centralizing its major agencies and activities, staffed with his own people, in Bogotá.

Roger Vekemans, a Belgian Jesuit, became a valuable and talented helper. Vekemans had been sent to Chile in the 1950s by Jesuit General Janssens at the request of Chilean bishops alarmed by growing leftist sentiment. There he threw his organizing talents behind the Christian Democrats in an effort to stop the socialist movements led by Salvador Allende. He quickly built up specialized institutes to train anticommunist leaders and create a theological, philosophical and sociological framework to justify his violent rejection of the then emerging Liberation Theology.

His apparently unlimited financial backing was soon a matter of public discussion and speculation. It was only in the mid-1970s, however, that documentation was published by the *Washington Star*, *Le Monde* (Paris) and the *National Catholic Reporter* tracing his funding to a network of reactionary forces, including the CIA. Aid was laundered through the DeRancé Foundation of Milwaukee, a major sponsor of traditionalist Catholic movements, and Aid to the Suffering Church headquartered in Italy and Switzerland. This organization, supported by European and North American business interests, stresses its help to Christians persecuted in communist countries. In fact, its main support is for extreme right-wing, vigilante-type activities in Latin America. (For an evaluation of Vekemans by leading German Catholic and Protestant theologians, see pp. 48ff.)

Vekeman's associations were so well identified by 1971 that when Allende won the presidential elections in Chile he sought a new base. His first choice was Caracas, but the Venezuelan government wanted no part of him. So he settled in Bogotá with the consent both of the ruling oligarchy and of Latin America's most conservative hierarchy. Joined almost immediately by López Trujillo, he quickly reestablished his research institutes, now centering his efforts on discrediting the Liberation Theology that he saw as the ideological underpinning of the progressives.

From the outset López Trujillo used his office very intelligently to promote his purposes. Concentrating his attack on the theology of liberation as ultimately subversive both of church and state, he urged the church everywhere to adopt instead the status quo role that characterized it in Colombia: to protect its own institutions, close ranks against the communist threat, and avoid internal conflicts. As a gift wrapping to give the package a progressive appearance, he stressed opposition to authoritarian regimes. This created no problem at home, because the ultra-reactionary Colombian regime maintains a crumbling democratic façade.

López Trujillo's attacks on the theology of liberation were supported not only by Vekemans but by such other conservative European theologians as Paul Dominique Dognin and Pierre Bigó. He also formed close alliances with reactionary elements in the Roman Curia, a strategy that paid off for him when the time came to plan the Puebla Conference. It so happened that the objectives of the curialists paralleled closely those of López Trujillo.

During Vatican II, the Roman Curia's assertion of authority to make church policy in the name of the pope was vigorously challenged. It became clear that a vast majority of the Council Fathers wanted the principle of collegiality institutionalized. This would make the bishops with the pope the determiners of policy, returning the Curia to its proper place as the permanent civil service implementing that policy. Pope Paul VI began the process by creating the Synod of Bishops to meet at established intervals and survey the needs of the church. The Curia, nevertheless, was able to prevent the acquisition by the Synod of the power the Council Fathers had sought for it. As Pope Paul grew older and more fearful of the danger of an open split in the church, the Curia by the mid-1970s had effectively recovered its primacy over the bishops.

Events in Latin America were of understandable concern to the Curia. An obvious reason was the absolute and relative increase in its Catholic population. The number of Catholics in the rest of the world is relatively declining. Europe in 1900 had more than 50 percent of all Catholics, today it has 37 percent, and it will have an even smaller percentage by the year 2000. In that year Latin America will have more than 50 percent of all Catholics, having grown from 20 percent in 1900 to 40 percent today.

In the late Middle Ages the Roman Curia concentrated power over the European church in itself by creating an ideological consensus that caused the dominated (the "ordinary faithful") to agree emotionally and psychologically with the dominators (the hierarchy). From that time, the people concurred in accepting a subordinate and passive status as the design of God and the teaching of Jesus. An essential role in transmitting this conditioning to the people was played by the rural pastor in a Europe that was then primarily rural. As Europe urbanized, the industrial workers escaped the pastor's thought control, and—not surprisingly—ceased to be church members.

Latin Americans, although overwhelmingly rural until recently, never established the European pastor relationship. One reason for this was the fewness of priests; another, the fact of huge areas thinly populated; and yet another, the existence of indigenous models (as noted earlier in reference to the grassroots communities) favoring a more horizontal and egalitarian structure. Efforts to impose the European pattern over the past thirty years, starting with Pope Pius XII's call for 30,000 foreign missionaries to "evangelize" a hemisphere sunk in "ignorance and superstition," simply have not worked.

What would work would be the traditional structures favored by López Trujillo and Vekemans. They would provide a concept of church as a regimented and embattled force in a hostile world, a church in which power had to be invested in the rulers—ultimately the Curia—and the role of the faithful would be to obey. The church of the liberation theologians growing out of the grassroots communities would seek collegial rather than hierarchical decison-making and would in consequence be a direct threat to the Curia's power. López Trujillo and his curial friends were in clear agreement that the attack must be centered on the theology of liberation. If it could be discredited, the rest would be easy.

The opening salvo was a "confidential" letter in May 1976 from López Trujillo to all Latin American bishops. In it he deplored the evils that follow the theology of liberation and its "distortion" of the message of Medellin. He centered on SAL (*Sacerdotes para América Latina*), the Colombian progressive priests' organization. Its membership was very small, he said. Most members were not priests. Some of the priest members were suspended or married. In addition, he continued, SAL promoted a Marxist ideology, attacked the church frequently, was allied to Christians for Socialism, and had powerful backers. Even if insignificant in itself, this kind of sickness is contagious. "There are various indications that similar groups who challenge authority are spreading in other countries."

These themes had already been developed in a meeting in Rome two months earlier. Liberation Theology, the international audience was told, is synonymous with Christians for Socialism, creates clerical militancy and disobedience, challenges national security, and inevitably leads to communism and atheism. The same themes were repeated at regional meetings of bishops in Bogotá, Rio de Janeiro, San José (Costa Rica), and San Juan (Puerto Rico). They were further reinforced by the mailing to all Latin American bishops of two books published by CEDIAL (*Centro de Estudios para el Desarrollo e Integración de América Latina*) of Bogotá, an organization founded and directed by Vekemans. The books, *Introducción a Karl Marx* by P.D. Dognin, and *Esperanzas Encontradas: Cristianismo y Marxismo* (Conflicting Hopes: Christianity and Marxism) by G. Cottier, are dedicated to the thesis that Christianity and Marxism are totally irreconcilable, and they call on all Latin Americans to join in the struggle against atheistic communism. The Ecumenical Council of Costa Rica described them as "a generous gift" to the bishops paid for with money from the United States, noting that one of them expressly acknowledged a subsidy from the DeRancé Foundation.

The influence of López Trujillo and Vekemans was also evident in the Synod of Bishops, Rome, October 1977. Although Cardinal Juan Landazuri of Lima, Peru, first vice-president at that time of CELAM, said flatly that Latin America's bishops cannot be manipulated by anyone, and that "Medellin is alive," most of the episcopal interventions were muted on the themes of injustice and repression. As *Vida Nueva*, an important Spanish Catholic review, put it: "Some of the statements sounded like Chinese to anyone with even a superficial knowledge of the reality of Latin America."

26

4. Evangelization: Indoctrination or Liberation

Within the framework of the reality of the Latin American church and society as already outlined, what are the concrete issues to which the bishops should give priority in their deliberations at Puebla?

The theme was set in December 1976 at a CELAM meeting in Puerto Rico: "Evangelization in the present and in the future of Latin America." Crucial to the development within and the outcome of the conference would be the bishops' concept of "evangelization." Equally important would be their perception of the present reality and convictions about the future. Such factual evidence as increased violence, the poor becoming poorer while the rich increase their surplus, more jobless and homeless, could not be ignored. Nor could the increased political activity among clerical leaders, and a movement among the marginated peoples toward an organized effort to assert themselves. The interpretation of these concrete realities would dictate the task assumed by the bishops chosen by their colleagues as their spokesmen. Both the evaluation and the future planning depend on their understanding of evangelization.

Today, as in the past, there are various interpretations of evangelization. As is well known, the Spaniards and Portuguese who colonized Latin America were Roman Catholic. The kind of evangelization their missionaries "adapted" was mass "conversion" of a purely formal nature. The natives were drilled in religious practices and a mechanical recitation of formulas, and then baptized. The personal incorporation into the life of Jesus Christ happened accidentally, if and when.

A few early missionaries succeeded in liberating themselves according to the model of Jesus.[1] One, Bartolomé de las Casas, seeing how the slaves were treated, spent his life pleading with Spain to cease the exploitation of the Indians and treat them as humans. The "encomienda" system had entrusted these natives to Spanish landlords, who assumed responsibility for making them "Christians," and forcing them to work "as a Christian should." His influence, like that of other like-minded liberators of his time, was limited by the combined forces of church and state whose vested interests were threatened. Those who today seek to reroot the Catholic faith in the Gospel point to such radicals as their precursors.

These new Roman Catholics learned their lessons well. The newborn continue today to be baptized; the graves of the dead are blessed. Feasts of the saints are celebrated with fervor; the virgin is honored; penitential practices are observed. Replicas of Jesus on the cross, as well as of Mary and the saints, adorn every home or hovel. Mass is attended with some regularity wherever it is available. Medals are worn, candles lit, and rosary beads used. All this confirms that Catholic indoctrination has been incorporated into the society and culture of nearly all native Americans and mestizos.

Given this background, one would think that when in 1976 the bishops chose evangelization as their primary concern, they had in mind something more than simple indoctrination. Some bishops, however, saw little prospect of changing the system. Understanding in their traditional theology that administration of the seven sacraments, divinely entrusted to them, is essential, they lacked personnel for anything else. And the future offered them no improvement. Rapidly increasing population, defection of priests and religious women, scarcity of vocations, and what has been called secularization of the culture—evident in a decrease in Mass attendance and reception of the sacraments—threatened the structure upon which their church as mediator is built. These bishops sought ways to stretch their declining priest population, or to adopt alternate means for the people to receive the sacramentalized service. Not an easy task. And few, if any, ready solutions.

Evangelization, if understood as the proclamation of a God whose love extends to all people, and who calls us into being as co-creators, presents a different challenge. How proclaim a just God who values each human person equally to the masses of people in a society deeply marked by inequality and injustice? How speak of the transformation wrought in all our lives through the good news of God's love to people in a society where one social class is exploited for the benefit of another? The community of those who practice the good news in solidarity with the poor, the basic sign of following Jesus, is a challenge to those structures. The church has a role only to the extent that it is such a community.[2]

The demands of the gospel are incompatible with the social situation of Latin America. To become a community of equals is impossible within the structures that determine human relationships. For God to be fleshed out in this history, it becomes necessary to fashion a completely different social order. Efforts toward social assistance or the simplistic ideal of "human betterment" are not enough. An authentic proclamation of God's love, human brotherhood, and total equality of everyone requires open recognition of the universal injustices and a commitment to end them.

Unfortunately, today the institutionalized "Christian" element is integrated into the prevailing ideology of domination, so that it lends support and cohesiveness to a capitalist society divided into classes. Conservative sectors appeal to Christian principles to justify the social order that serves their interests and maintains their privileges.

Many influential church members and leaders have long been closely tied to the unjust social order. The conscientization now being effected through the *comunidades de base* has set in motion a process of evangelization that forces believers to liberate themselves. Newly conscious of their rights as human persons, they feel the need to embody their faith in a political struggle to enforce these rights. The church being born of the people—which includes bishops and clergy—will proclaim the gospel of good news to the poor, the same gospel that is bad news for the rich and the powerful.[3]

Such was the task facing the bishops as they prepared for Puebla. The question was: How many were ready to deal with it? Many had "missed" Vatican II's call repeated at Medellin. They sought to steer the church on its traditional course in its traditional forms; structurally, a pyramid of power, stressing religious practices, seeing itself as an international institution, the universal instrument of salvation. They perceived the church as possessing the truth and themselves as divinely assigned to give this truth to the people whose function was limited to obeying. Their duty was to guard the faith and protect the people.

Other bishops, the most vocal being the Brazilians, had a different dream. The church was for them in process among the people, with horizontal structures, understanding itself as a community rather than a society. They wanted to share the people's struggle to become more human. Instead of dispensing salvation already possessed, they sought to enflesh the living God in today's reality. Salvation would be realized when "the blind receive their sight and the lame walk, lepers are cleansed and the deaf hear, the dead are raised up, and the poor have the good news preached to them" (Matt. 11:5).[4]

Professing these radically different ecclesiologies the Latin American bishops nevertheless acknowledged their appointment to power or to service—dependent upon their self-concept—by the Supreme Pontiff of the one Roman Catholic

Church. Accepting their individual "good faith," we turn to their personal theologies—their understanding of God—to make sense of their conflicting stances.

The conservatives believe in a provident God who created the universe, who takes care of everything, and who—because he is just—will mysteriously balance the scale in the end. The believer is not to question experience but to "accept the will of God."[5] The reality of hunger, of violence, of human misery, is inconsequential, because "God is not of this world." Jesus' death and resurrection pay the price of human sin and reopen the gates of heaven for those who choose to live with God in eternity. The church interprets God's will, mediates between God and humankind.

The progressives proclaim a God continually involved with and in the world. This God of the Exodus united with oppressed peoples against the oppressor and made concrete the invitation to humans to total liberation in the person of Jesus. This Jesus of history who dies in conflict with the powerful of his time yet continues to live offers people an alternative to oppression. Freedom or liberation is not only God's gift—a basic human right—but also possible. Jesus removed the need for a mediator, offering us equal access to our basic rights. The church is the community of those who believe in life over death and stand before the world as a symbol of this reality. In this church, according to Bishop Anibal Maricevich Fleitas of Concepcion, Paraguay, "the people and the bishops are to be brothers and servants of the poor."

The bishops representing these two concepts of church (with their corresponding concepts of God) were the principals at Puebla. Would they face the issues? Would they attempt to design a plan to indoctrinate the masses or one to assist the people in total human liberation? The poor may be understood as the special ones who are destined to suffer in this life, or as persons subjected to an unjust system. The rich may be reminded of their responsibility to "feed the hungry" or confronted with the bad news of the difficulty of threading a needle with a camel.

Liberation Theology, as already noted, was the up-front issue. Those who feared the prospect of massive groups of people standing up to proclaim their own liberation and assert their rights were quick to note the departure from traditional theology. An assertion of equal right to the means of life is easily misinterpreted by those who fear any socialist solution. A ready way to discredit the entire approach is to focus on the "atheistic" teaching of Marx, overlooking John XXIII's distinction in *Pacem in Terris* between false philosophical principles and the concrete socio-economic systems that have evolved from them.[6] This approach also ignores the experience of Cuba where people enjoy food, clothing, shelter, and work, and where the church in consequence stands helpless as it searches for a new raison d'être.[7]

What we have described are basically the two extremes of the broad spectrum of theological, pastoral, and political attitudes coexisting in uneasy equilibrium within the Latin American hierarchy. It would not be easy to establish a consensus as to what adaptations the church needed to make it more functional today and tomorrow, or as to what stands it should take in the face of the rapidly changing society.

How, for example, should it deal with the shortage of priests? Would it consider the possibility of ordaining married men or of ordaining women? Would it look to the *comunidades de base* as the key to a thriving church with a minimum of "official" ministers and a maximum of collegial sharing of responsibility and service?

Would it limit its evaluation of social change to a general protest against the existing evils, violence, counterviolence, torture, dictatorial governments monopolizing power under the neofascist doctrine of national security, masses of unemployed and starving while global corporations exported fat profits? Or would it go beyond a laundry list of the visible evils to search for the systemic causes? And beyond general condemnation of injustice to point the finger directly at Nicaragua, El Salvador, Argentina, Chile and other regimes whose systematic violation of citizens' rights had been amply documented by Amnesty International and other wholly reliable sources? Would it ask the institutional church to "change sides," pointing out that historically it has been on the side of the rich, whereas the gospel directs it to be on the side of the poor?

The Preliminary Document (PD), first draft of a working paper sent in late 1977 by CELAM to all Latin American bishops, suggested answers to some of these questions. As we shall see, many found its answers inadequate.

5. The Issues as Formulated by CELAM

The stated purpose of the Preliminary Document (PD) was to review the Latin American reality and set the tone for the upcoming meeting. It was an amazing production, 214 dreary pages, verbose, repetitive, dull, lifeless, shallow, self-contradictory. Efforts were made to keep its contents secret, but a secret shared with many hundreds of people is never a secret for long. As copies of the PD became available, the reaction was stunning. Soon hundreds of thousands of words of evaluation and criticism were being published in magazines, newspapers, newsletters, pamphlets. Responses came from all Latin America, from the United States and Canada, and from the other continents.[1]

Not only Catholics, not only Christians, not only believers, but all concerned with the dignity and value of people were demonstrating that Puebla would be a key moment in the life of the church and civilization. All these were shocked and frustrated by the PD which, instead of a prophecy, offered an exercise in housecleaning and navel-gazing. Fear, intellectualism, and defense against danger dominate the document. Joy in the midst of suffering, faith in the Lord's resurrection of a massacred people, hope in the struggle revealed in the liberation of the oppressed, all are absent from the lifeless pages.

The PD cut at the very heart of Medellin, the event that,

34

according to Chilean priest Segundo Galilea, "captured the 'soul' of the church and the Latin American people".[2] The document's interpretation of the Latin American reality and its definition of the church's task do not correspond to the religious experience and theological reflection of the Christian communities throughout the continent.

It is obvious that the authors of the document have not exposed themselves to the experience and pastoral reflection of base groups. This lack of roots explains the distortions, contradictions and silences—however subtle—evident in the PD. Noted particularly are the fear of facing up to the condition of the poor and a failure to see their role in the evangelizing task.

A tragic example of the betrayal of Medellin in the PD is found in what is said and not said regarding the concept of the poor. After affirming that "In Latin America there are very many poor people" (650), "a broad meaning" (651) is enlisted to define the term poor. The text then uses a number of nuances, interpretations and meanings to arrive at "a concept of the poor that is creative and complex" (653). A distinction between material and spiritual poverty is attempted, thus making everyone and no one poor. Since, then, the "very many" poor do not exist, they do not have to be dealt with.

Confronted with the Medellin document which focuses on the poor, the PD inserted such statements as: "The gospel makes it urgent for us to contribute to the creation of an economic and political order where justice and freedom reign and in which the poor are authentic protagonists" (711). This excellent statement is in direct conflict with an exhortation to conformism and resignation that appears earlier in the same document: "By evangelizing them and receiving them into its bosom, the church makes poor people participants in a supreme home, founded on the promises of the Lord. Even when they are deprived of everything, they possess the richness of having a God, who being rich became poor (II Cor. 8:9), and faith, as a word that nourishes, lets them live with fortitude

35

and the joy of the Kingdom, already embryonic, which no human pain can take away" (657).

At Medellin, the protagonist of history is the poor; it is the oppressed who challenge the church to define its mission. The protagonist of the PD is the people, rich and poor, treated as a whole. The common characteristic of this people is the culture. The great problem, then, becomes the secularization of the culture, not the oppression of the poor. The defined culture is Western. The "cultures of silence"—Indians, Blacks, and natives of Latin America—on which the so-called Latin American version of Western culture has been imposed, are scarcely mentioned.[3]

The PD uses the modernizing project as its intermediary to stake out the ground for its general problem of secularism and a questioning of the faith. It attempts to accept the values of industrialization and technology while rejecting secularism, which according to the document's authors "has unfortunately already begun to exercise its influence in Latin America." Modernization is treated in an abstract way. Nothing is said of the bourgeois social class that stimulates industrialization within the dependent capitalism of Latin America. The domination and exploitation of the lower classes are intensified by an economic model that supports national and international interests. Yet the PD points to "a new civilization" where a movement to an urban-industrial society will occur without detriment to the Christian values. According to the document, "Western culture has been built upon this faith in the revelation of a provident God" (357). Therefore, Western and Christian go together.

A basic assumption made is that challenges come from ideologies, not from reality. However, the exploitation of the masses is the fact that radically calls into question the life and reflection of the church in Latin America. Such is the belief that supported all those who have given their lives in commitment to the struggles of the poor, which the document ignores.

The PD chooses as its battlefield the Western European world, judging Latin America to be merely its reflection.

Nothing is said of the social costs of industrialization. While the multinational corporations are rebuked for not having a "just view of the common good," they are thanked for having "increased the production of the companies with their advanced technology and improved working conditions and workingmen's wages" (195). This statement again reveals the lack of awareness of the reality of a continent in which conditions grow progressively worse, with fewer jobs and lower wages. To be quiet about all this is to be an accomplice of the vested interests that the bourgeois class defends. External dependence is admitted, though pointedly as "not the only" factor.

The solutions offered, as though coming from a caring father, are honesty, austerity, and savings! All are "virtues" well known to the poor. The patience implied is long overdrawn. Being in touch with the liberating gospel of Jesus Christ, who confronted his enemies, is the hope and the faith that enable the poor to reject pious platitudes in favor of acts that will bring them what is rightfully theirs.

Among the more insidious undercurrents in the document is that Vatican II and Medellin completed the updating of the church in Latin America. It is implied that the objectives sought have been achieved and that the church can consequently return to its traditional resting place in the sacristy, confident that it has reformed society.

The reality is that the objectives proposed by Medellin in 1968 have not been achieved, either regarding the internal life of the church itself or regarding the reforms required before Latin American society could be called minimally Christian. All the distortions described by Medellin have grown exponentially in ten years.[4] The task now is not just to redescribe but to devote the same effort to the search for solutions that Medellin devoted to the diagnosis.

The suggestion that oppressors and the oppressed can co-exist in one community (here the community of the church) is a theme dear to the United States and others who benefit from existing inequalities. Institutionalized violence of the oppressor and the survival counterviolence of the oppressed cannot be equated. They are not equally condemnable and equally to blame for the failure of society to prosper. It also contradicts Medellin which had stated forthrightly that violence does not appear when the first gun is fired, but when the first act of injustice takes place, and that those who attempt to retain inordinate wealth and power are responsible for provoking explosive revolutions of despair.[5]

The institutional church is presented in the PD as constantly taking the lead in the definition and protection of human rights. Historically, only isolated individuals, often repudiated by the hierarchy, protested the domesticating role of the institution and its distortion of the consciences of the oppressors. For how many church leaders have Antonio de Montesinos, Bartolomé de las Casas, Miguel Hidalgo or José María Morelos been a living memory, an inspiration, or a challenge?

The classical neoscholastic theology of the document deals with three important concepts: God, the person of Jesus, and the church. God is the "providential God." To believe in this God is to have faith that "the Lord is not a passive but active God, supernaturally present in the world, and that the world is not unaffected by this divine action." Given the abundance of negatives, this passage minimizes the action of God in history for Christians in Latin America who have a vigorous awareness of the action and presence of the Lord in history. A similar minimizing results from speaking of God as "supernaturally present."

In much the same way, Jesus appears divested of his own history. The rich personal experience of a Jesus who dies in conflict with the powerful of his time is emptied and reembodied as the incarnation of a transcendent God. The lines dedicated to the resurrection (417, 419, 484, 487) come dry from a textbook, rather than flowing from the paschal experience of a believing, oppressed, and massacred people. Today's martyrs, for the poor the true witnesses of resurrection, are ignored.

We see a return to the vertical and pyramidal power relationships in the PD's vision of the church. The bishops are the hierarchy who stand above and watch over the people. The history of evangelization in Latin America is documented only by the bishops' meetings and councils, with no reference to those who daily give their lives in the struggle for the rights of the people.

The *comunidades de base*, the church of the people that stands out visibly as a witness to the liberating power of the gospel, are not mentioned. Their exclusion was a "happy fault." This, more than anything else, caused the document to be carefully read, making it impossible for other propaganda to slip through.

The strength and hope of the church in Latin America come through loud and clear in the people's response to the document. They did not lose heart. They looked upon the manner of treating the subjects proposed as arbitrary. It was only a text for discussion. The president of CELAM, Cardinal Aloisio Lorscheider, placed some valuable guidelines for dialogue when he said: "The climate and the message of the III Conference are to be the communication of the good news in joyous, optimistic, and realistic preaching which is fitting for pastors who in humility and simplicity base their hope on the power of the spirit". And later he said: "The concrete history of Latin America is the horizon on which the deliberations and orientation of the III Conference will be written."[6]

Time and again throughout the PD there recurs the innuendo that Protestantism (always preceded by the adjective "liberal") is a root cause of Latin America's malaise. For at least a century up to 30 years ago, Protestantism was the convenient whipping boy for everything that went wrong with the

Catholic Church in Latin America.[7] Happily, Vatican II purged us of that error and opened our eyes to the deep spiritual and Christian values our fellow Christians are happy to share with us. It is unrealistic to try to resurrect the prejudice of yesteryear. Like Christendom, anti-Protestantism lies dead in its unmarked, unmourned grave.

It is an illusion to imagine—as the PD does—that the solution requires a return to a theology that is antiquated and repudiated. There is no possibility of a new Christendom,[8] nor would it be desirable. Secularization is not only a reality but a positive one. The function of the church, as Vatican II made clear, is to be a servant of humanity, a leaven in the world, a sacramental sign of Christ's presence and the support of the spirit in the common effort to bring the world to the perfection God intended for it.[9]

Remembering that the document was written by men sharing the views of López Trujillo, it is not surprising that Lorscheider's perspective is missing. The laity, religious, priests and bishops who live and work among the exploited people placed their trust in Lorscheider and others like him who comprehend the demands of the Spirit for a church that wants to put down its roots among these people.

The PD, delivered in December 1977, alerted those conscious of the cost and the reward of achieving liberation to the need for true evangelization of the church hierarchy. The road to Puebla appeared long and treacherous. Committed as they were to Medellin, there was for them no option. They did not seek to create a new church but to ensure that the one church of Jesus remain always faithful to the good news he proclaims.

6. The People of God Challenge CELAM's Formulation

During the summer of 1978 the bishops of each country of Latin America met to evaluate the Preliminary Document and offer suggestions and comments to be forwarded to the CELAM secretariat as input to a revised Working Document (WD). The CELAM authorities had decided that the staff assigned to draft the WD would ignore all comments from any source other than those received from the bishops' conferences. This was in line with the unformulated but obvious intention that Puebla should be an assembly of bishops, not an ecclesial reunion like Medellin where the whole People of God was directly involved through theologians and other spokespeople.

Many of the national conferences, nevertheless, sought the broadest participation of the people and took serious note of their views in drafting their replies to the PD. Of primary importance was the response from the grassroots communities, because they showed the church as alive among the poor, and because they insisted on their confidence that the church would not abandon them in their plight at a time when all other pretended defenders and supporters had failed them. How extensive that input was can be instanced by the fact that the bishops of Chile received and studied 6,000 communications from grassroots communities when preparing their response, this in a country where repression was such that membership in any kind of grassroots organization was a risk.[1]

The responses from Chile and elsewhere dealt with a vast array of different problems, but they all came back ultimately to the central issue that the people of Latin America face. They were looking to the church to proclaim liberation and to lead them in their struggle to liberate themselves.

"We are undernourished and hungry," they pleaded. "Most of us are illiterate. Our housing and health conditions are shockingly bad. Unemployment is alarmingly high and increasing. We live in an exploited and oppressed continent, subject to torture, the women also subject to violation and forced into prostitution. We are denied our political and trade-union rights. Everyone else has abandoned us. Do not you, our fathers in God, abandon us. At least, start us on our journey to the Promised Land."

The pathos, the faith, the hope of hundreds of such cries from people regarded by all too many of us as lacking the ability to formulate any logical or abstract concept is simply incredible. Among the many we have studied, one has affected us more than any other. It was written in their native Guaraní by peasants of the diocese of Coronel Oviedo, Paraguay. Perhaps our special emotional response to this document has been affected by the fact that one of us has had the privilege of seeing the conditions in which these peasants live, of having been welcomed into their homes, shared their simple food, and drunk the *maté* that is passed from hand to hand to be shared by all present as an expression of respect and friendship. Here are some of the more striking passages from their appeal for support in their 30-year struggle against the repression and despoliation of one of the world's most ruthless dictatorships.

"Previously in our religious life, we believed that all our personal, family, community and social sufferings were divine tests that we had to endure and even offer up for the glory of

God and our sanctification. We bore them with fervor and joy, even when they were destructive of our lives and those of our families.

"How often have we buried our children resignedly in the belief that God needed them as angels in heaven! How often have we fallen down fainting from hunger when working our tiny plots! . . .

"But God in his great goodness and justice caused his word to reach some of our brothers, 'little prophets' of the people. With Bible in hand, they began to discover there was a different face of God. A just and good God, who even has a Plan of Salvation, prepared at the beginning of history for all people. They learn and begin to communicate to others that God has always walked side by side with us, and a living sign of this was the coming of Christ to make clear and strengthen the Plan of Salvation. God does not desire human suffering. In the Plan we find justice, love of our neighbor, and as the goal, human happiness. Joined by some priests, we began on this basis to practice a life of mutual love, now with an awareness that God was not to blame for our misfortunes and sufferings.

"In this process of mutual help, we began to dialogue and to undertake joint agricultural efforts. We organized a consumer cooperative as a tangible proof of our desire to help each other and as one way to solve our problems. But our initiative was received badly in some places, and charges began to circulate that we were Protestants, communists, opposed to the government. Next came persecution, threats, jailings, tortures, destruction of our cooperative centers. Those who accused us most harshly were the merchants.

"At times, when by some chance a newspaper reached us, we learned that peasants like us, both in our country and elsewhere in Latin America, were suffering the same repression and injustice. For example, the heads of the families of an entire settlement would be jailed because the land had been sold out from under them to a person of power; and usually the end

43

result was the expulsion of all the people who had worked the land for years, with many held in jail to intimidate them. (Many of us who are writing you have been imprisoned and finally released without any charges being brought against us.)

"When we learned that the bishops were to meet at Medellin, ten years ago, we sent a report to them about our shocking situation and told them how great were our hopes that they would take our needs into account. Soon there began to arrive, like a life-giving rain, the news that the bishops were indeed taking us into account, that they recognized us as a fundamental part of the church, that our sufferings and persecutions were felt by the whole church; that in a word, not God but men were the cause of our unhappy situation. They also made clear to us that the accumulation of wealth in the hands of a few permits the creation of a society structured to preserve and protect the privileged situation of that group, and that a solution could result only from a change of the structure of that unjust society, replacing it with a structure based on the Gospel. . . .

"The enthusiasm and drive generated by the bishops came up against a more continuous and generalized repression that used all means at hand without scruple. The clear intervention of the bishops in their documents in support of the justice of our claims soon began to decline in practice. Many of our companions gave up the struggle when no quick solution was found for our problems, fearing they would lose more rather than achieve anything. The response of most of our bishops and priests was the same, a gradual withdrawal.

"We are now isolated and the authorities are using every means to persecute us. They have invaded our communities, destroyed our work bases, forced us to abandon our homes, subjected us to long imprisonments. They now control all our movements and keep us under constant surveillance. . . .

"We have learned that some bishops now say that the situation of injustice made known at Medellin has been overcome. We assure you, respected bishops, that here in our country the same state of injustice—and even worse—continues. The fact is that there are a few who grow constantly richer, while we poor people grow more numerous and are driven ever deeper into misery. We understand that a document is circulating in our country whose clear purpose is to undo what Medellin did. . . .

"We believe that the projects designed to change the structures must be put into effect. The church itself should set the example, starting the radical institutional changes that are needed to perform more effectively the mission entrusted to it by Christ.

"We are concerned about the situation of priests and religious who withdraw from their priestly work. The cause of their leaving is not vocational but institutional. It results from two problems that seriously weaken the church as institution and have repercussions on all its members. One is the blocking of their efforts to engage in serious pastoral work with the people. The other is celibacy.

"We believe it necessary to have the conclusions of the Pastoral Consultation put into effect, a process to which all of us contributed, in part with our ideas, in part with our way of living.

"It is necessary and urgent to ordain as deacons the committed laymen who are willing, this as a first step toward ordination of married men to the priesthood, that is to say, the abolition of obligatory celibacy.

"We believe these measures will be the first steps in a deep structural change to enable the church to rise out of its stagnation and be the light and the efficacious mover for realizing the salvific plan of God for humankind. . . .

"We end with an expression of our great hope that these reflections and suggestions of ours may reach you and be taken into account by you. We are church, and we want to feel united with you bishops, our pastors."[2]

Various national conferences made their responses public. As they became known, they restored the hope of the many who had been saddened by the tone and thrust of the PD. Particularly remarkable was the reply of the bishops of Colombia who were universally recognized as the most reactionary and unresponsive in Latin America, if not in the whole world.[3]

Awakened from their slumbers, the Colombian bishops acknowledged that "a tremendous moral crisis" had engulfed national life, the "insatiable appetite for quick riches" being such as to have perverted every sector of society, even the armed forces, so that contraband, narcotics traffic, and every kind of fraud flourish. The economic structures had become untenable, with low wages, unemployment and underemployment. Economic, social, and political inequalities had produced the greatest concentration of wealth in a few hands of any Latin American country, while more than a quarter of the people lived in extreme poverty with annual income of less than US $75.

Not content with merely analyzing the existential reality of the poor, something they had already done fully, especially in three collective statements from the bishops of the North-East, Amazonia, and the North-West, the bishops of Brazil urged Puebla to lead in liberating action.[4] They called for even more effort throughout the hemisphere to promote the grass-roots church communities which they recognized as constituting one of the most dynamic features in their church. They opted for a church of brotherhood, participation, and dialogue, open study of divisive issues, and a priority concern—though not an exclusive one—for the poor. And they stressed the duty of the church to raise the consciousness of all its members so that they become aware of the scandal of the tremendous injustices that exist in a continent claiming the name of Christian.

Many organizations cooperated in collecting and diffusing the enormous flood of reflections and observations that came from the most diverse sources, many from outstanding theologians, others from the hovels of the poor. Three groups in Mexico City played key parts: CENCOS (*Centro Nacional de Comunicación Social*: National Center of Social Communication), CRIE (*Centro Regional de Informaciones Ecuménicas*: Regional Center of Ecumenical News), and *Christus* magazine.[5] CENCOS and CRIE both opened centers at Puebla that were of enormous help to the journalists from all parts of the world. CENCOS, headed by the indefatigable José Alvarez Icaza, in addition to daily bulletins, organized conferences and interviews. Alvarez Icaza participated in the Vatican Council with his wife as representing the Christian family, and he was subsequently for many years a member of the Vatican Council for the Laity. In what some interpreted as an effort to cool his ardor for social justice and reduce his input into the preparations for the Puebla Conference, the police one day in 1978 carted him and a half dozen fellow workers off to jail, ransacked the offices and carried off all equipment and invaluable reference files. It took several days of national and international protests to have them released and some of their seized property returned. But "Pepe," as he is universally known, refused to be intimidated.

Another important contribution was an entire issue of the prestigious United States quarterly review *Cross Currents*, with contributions from Latin America, the United States, and Canadian theologians, stressing the importance of Puebla not only for the church in Latin America but for the universal church. The Rome-based International Documentation and Communication Center (IDOC) similarly brought together the reflections of major European theologians and published them in the principal European languages.

Particularly noteworthy in the *Cross Currents* issue was an article by a United Methodist minister, Dow Kirkpatrick, on what Puebla can do for Protestants in the United States. Kirkpatrick is officially engaged in "reverse mission," seeking

47

to interpret to his church members in the United States the reality of Latin America and the impact of the United States on its condition. As members of a rich society, he said, which inevitably seeks to maintain its affluence, they need "an affirmation of the church of the poor" to break out of their slavery to the consumer society. "Hope for liberation of the rich comes as a gift from the poor. . . . We need help to qualify ourselves for the benefit of the beatitudes."

Two other important statements in this review were an open letter signed by several hundred prominent North Americans, including leading Catholic and Protestant theologians, and an open letter from a group of Germany's most prominent Catholic and Protestant theologians. The North Americans stressed how important Puebla would be for religion in the United States. "What we have learned from you over the last decade is vitally important to our own growth toward the fullness of life in Jesus Christ. Following your initiative at Medellin, we too are discovering that the Gospel takes on an entirely new meaning for us when we read it through the eyes of the poor. We, too, are recognizing the dimension of credibility and authenticity in that style of episcopal leadership which grows from identification with the poor at the base."

The German theologians included such universally known figures as Karl Rahner, Herbert Vorgrimler, Johannes B. Metz, Norbert Greenscher, Walter Dirks, Martin Niemoller, Helmut Gollwitzer, Ernst Kasemann, and Paulus Engelhardt. The charges they made were very specific, as some extracts will make clear.

"Evidence is multiplying that the campaign conducted by influential circles of the Catholic church of Federal Germany against the theology of liberation and many Latin American movements close to it, which has been going on for some time, is becoming so virulent that we must make a public protest. We the signers of this memorandum are convinced that this not very brotherly attack is a threat that endangers autonomous church evolution in Latin America, something that began at Medellin (1968), and is causing divisions between theologians and bishops in the national churches. We intend to point out some aspects of the campaign, and in particular call attention to the regrettable alliance between the administrators of *Adveniat*, the German bishops' funding agency, and Father Roger Vekemans, known in Latin America as a declared enemy of the theology of liberation. . . .

"Vekemans is director of the Center of Studies for Development and Integration in Latin America (CEDIAL), in Bogotá, Colombia. He has not only distinguished himself by his untiring action in Latin America and Europe against the theology of liberation, but has also become an ambiguous figure after the press accused him of having received millions of dollars of subsidy from the CIA to support imperialist policies in Latin America. (Cf. *The Washington Star*, July 23, 1975; *Le Monde*, July 23, 27, 28, 1975.)

"For many priests and Christians in Latin America it is clear that Vekemans has not only received large grants from such church organizations as *Adveniat*, but he also made use of his influence and key role in many governing boards and organizations to get the support of groups (like Opus Dei) that are politically useful to him, groups which at the same time deny equally generous support to many who are working for the self-liberation of poor and oppressed people.

"On the part of the Latin American episcopacy, the campaign against the theology of liberation is supported by Colombian bishops Alfonso López Trujillo (auxiliary, Bogotá and Dario Castrillón (Pereira). For this López Trujillo can exert considerable potential since he is also secretary of the Latin American Bishops' Council (CELAM). On the part of the Germans, those who are prominent in this campaign are Bishop Hengsbach (Essen), member of the board of directors of Adveniat, and professors Weber, Rauscher, and Bossle. . . .

"A study group they formed organized a costly colloquium in Rome, March 2–6, 1976, under the direction of Bishops Hengsbach and López Trujillo, largely financed by the West German church. Among the principal speakers besides the directors were Castrillón, Vekemans, Rauscher, and Weber. . . . It declared as its principal enemies the theology of liberation and the related movement of Christians for Socialism, both of which are reproached for having taken as their own a Marxist analysis of society and for having thereby undermined the Christian faith. . . .

"Many Latin American bishops have already expressed a concern that behind these statements there is hidden a tendency to mobilize the CELAM assembly to adopt the condemnation of the theology of liberation prepared by the circle close to López Trujillo. The position of Bishop Hengsbach, which conflicts with most of the Latin American bishops, is not the only striking thing in this affair. . . . During a trip to Latin America, the government of Bolivia decorated him with Bolivia's highest honor, the Condor of the Andes. Thus the attention of the German people is euphemistically diverted from the fact that the ill-famed dictator Banzer is at the head of this government. This decoration takes on even more grotesque features when it is seen in the context of a CIA document published in 1975, in which the following instructions were given to the Bolivian police: 'Only the church's progressive sector is to be attacked, not the church as an institution or the bishops as a group. . . . We should insistently repeat that they preach armed struggle, that they are linked with international communism, and that they were sent to Bolivia with the sole purpose of moving the church toward communism.' . . .

"Are the forces of the German church that support this campaign against the theology of liberation really aware of which interests they represent by this, or how they jeopardize the Latin American church, and of how much new suffering their attitude brings to priests and Christians who already must suffer enough under the yoke of military dictatorships?

We cannot serenely allow the German church again to fall under the grave suspicion of being on the side of the powerful, overlooking—consciously or not—the inhuman behavior of dictators who call themselves Christian, or interpreting it benevolently for tactical reasons. Therefore, we firmly demand the immediate suspension of any kind of backing for the campaign against the theology of liberation."

Simultaneously, the flow of events in Latin America during 1978 brought the real issues into sharper relief than ever before. The massive propaganda lies of the military dictatorships regarding the "miracles" of progress were revealed for what they were by one authoritative study after another. Independent, impartial investigators confirmed the institutionalized use of torture, the internments, the exiling of political opponents, the countless thousands of "disappeared" persons in Argentina, Chile, Guatemala, and elsewhere. At an accelerating rate, priests and nuns who identified with the victims of oppression were tortured, killed, or exiled. One episode in particular summarized and symbolized the state of the hemisphere: the massacre at Panzos, Guatemala, May 29. As confirmed by the clergy of the diocese of Verapaz, Indian men, women, and children coming for a peaceful discussion with the authorities were slaughtered to the number of more than a hundred by soldiers under the control of the big landholders who wanted the land of the Indians.[6] The hemisphere-wide and worldwide revulsion at this massacre raised the hopes of many that the bishops at Puebla would—in the words of a group of Peruvian theologians—proclaim "the resurrection in Christ of a massacred people."

Further encouragement for those who hoped Puebla would respond realistically to the needs of the oppressed and persecuted was given by Cardinal Aloisio Lorscheider, president of CELAM, in a talk to a group of German church leaders in Aachen, Germany, in September. He made four major points.[7]

1. The church in Latin America must continue to give primary importance to work with the poor. It must remain on the course for which it has already opted, namely, to identify with the poor and share their sufferings and hopes. In this he was reaffirming what the bishops of the Bolivarian countries (Peru, Bolivia, Ecuador, Colombia, Venezuela) said in their joint response to the PD: "We have reaffirmed in the light of the Gospel the truth that the poor are the first entitled to receive, and also the first agents of salvation." The stress on the active part the poor play in the process of their salvation is noteworthy.

2. The church must continue to raise its prophetic voice, making known and understood in every situation the prophetic contribution of the church to building a more human world.

3. Continued development of the grassroots communities, the most important new element in the life of the church in Latin America, should be given top priority among the many works of the church in all countries.

4. CELAM III should take into account and reflect in its statements the fact that by the end of this century Latin America will contain more than half the world's Catholics. In consequence, it must begin to adopt a very different self-image from that of the past when it was a receiver of missionaries from abroad. Now it is its turn to start to prepare for its role as a missionary church for the rest of the world.

López Trujillo was understandably concerned at the obviously widespread criticism of his PD, and he used the substantial resources at his disposal to counter the criticisms and to silence or discredit the critics. He was particularly annoyed by the exposés of his scheming in the Spanish Catholic weekly *Vida Nueva*. Having made several unsuccessful efforts to have Cardinal Enrique y Tarancón of Madrid to silence the editor, he made a special trip to Spain to develop a newspaper campaign of defamation of *Vida Nueva*, reportedly helped in this campaign by Opus Dei.

His primary concern, however, was to prepare a Working Document (WD) that would meet some of the criticisms of the bishops' conferences regarding the PD, but without changing the direction in which he sought to take the meeting. Realizing that it had been a tactical mistake to release the PD far enough ahead to allow wide discussion and development of unfavorable public opinion, he decided to hold the WD until the last moment before the opening of the Conference scheduled to meet October 12. In this way he hoped the bishops would assemble with only his work to influence them in their deliberations. As will emerge shortly, fate was to play a bad trick on him.

7. Ground Rules for the Conference

The Conference of the Latin American Bishops, like the Synod of Bishops and many other church assemblies, suffers from lack of clearly defined rules of procedure. In practice, some anonymous group generally referred to as "higher authority" makes the rules and changes them without any process of democratic consultation.

For the Puebla meeting, by this obscure process, three co-presidents were chosen and entrusted with the task of formulating ad hoc rules. They were Cardinal Aloisio Lorscheider of Fortaleza, Brazil, president of CELAM, Cardinal Sebastiano Baggio of the Roman Curia "representing the pope," and Archbishop Ernesto Corripio Ahumada of Mexico City. Lorscheider was well known for his progressive views. His evaluation of what he expected from Puebla, as set out in the preceding chapter, is typical of his thinking. But he is a humble person and in poor health. As events were to show, he was completely overshadowed by Baggio and Corripio Ahumada, both of them in total accord with López Trujillo and equally autocratic in their way of dealing with opposition and criticism.

One significant change in the rules concerned the selection of delegates. Previously each bishops' conference elected one delegate for each five or fewer members. This time the rule was modified to provide that conferences with more than a hundred members would have only one delegate for each ten members in excess of a hundred. The only country significantly affected was Brazil which has some three hundred bishops. Its hierarchy is overwhelmingly progressive, so that the effect of the change of rules was to reduce the progressive presence at Puebla.

The CELAM secretariat released four lists of participants and invitees during the months preceding the scheduled opening. The first list had 187 names. It included 177 bishops elected by their fellow bishops, 4 bishops named by Rome, and the top officers of the Latin American conference of men and women religious (CLAR).

How or why the 12 bishops in the second list were chosen has never been revealed, and the same is true for those on the third and fourth lists. In contrast with the 177 elected bishops, who reflected the wide range from ultraconservative to highly progressive within the entire episcopal body of Latin America, these 12 bishops were all either conservative or extremely conservative, the consequence being that they tilted the balance that the elections had achieved. They included Bogotá's Cardinal and Army General Muñoz Duque; Bishop Juan Fresno, supporter of Chile's military junta; and Bishop Alcides Mendoza Castro, religious head of Peru's armed forces. All are sympathetic to the doctrine of national security that justifies the monopoly of judgment by the armed forces and the destruction of democratic processes and the rule of law.

The third list of 84 included *periti* (theological experts), other priests, religious and lay people. The most striking quality of this list was the absence of every single one of the world-renowned exponents of contemporary Latin American theology, including those who had advised the bishops at Medellin and drafted its documents: Gustavo Gutiérrez, Juan L. Segundo, Leonardo Boff, Hugo Assmann, Jon Sobrino, Ignacio Ellacuria, Raúl Vidales, Enrique Dussel, Segundo Galilea, Pablo Richard, and many others.

Instead there were 20 theologians and social scientists, most of them unknown, all of them conservative, and nearly all—including Renato Poblete, Boaventura Kloppenburg, and Pierre Bigó—openly hostile to the theology of liberation. Kloppenburg and Bigó are Europeans, excluding the possibility that the highly Latin-Americanized José Comblin, a major force at Medellin, was passed over because of his Belgian birth. From Peru, instead of Gutiérrez, came the completely unknown Enrique Bartara. From Uruguay, instead of Segundo, Methol Ferre, known for a reactionary manichaeism unequalled in modern times.

The 48 priests, deacons, and lay people were similarly named without going through public consultative processes. Nearly all the priests were known for their conservative attitudes. And from Guatemala to represent the laity, 70 percent of whom are Indians oppressed and impoverished by local and foreign business, comes J. Skinner Klee, resident representative of the transnational enterprise Helena Rubenstein. Protests to Rome and to CELAM from Guatemala and elsewhere that cheeks of Christians should be red at the insult without need of cosmetics were ignored.

The fourth list included some cardinals, heads of some religious orders, an assortment of Europeans, and a few North Americans. Significantly, it omitted the head of the Congregation of Religious, Cardinal Eduardo Pironio, a doubly curious omission because Pironio is an Argentine and because more than half of all priests in Latin America are religious. It also omitted another staunch progressive, Jesuit General Pedro Arrupe. Instead, it included Father Werenfried van Straaten (who doesn't even merit a listing in the encyclopedic Vatican Yearbook, the *Annuario Pontificio*), founder and head of Aid to the Suffering Church. Exploiting popular sentiment for Christians persecuted in Eastern Europe after World War II, this organization has used major funds to support stridently anticommunist and even fascist-leaning groups in Latin America. Van Straaten has been seen in Holland in the company of the rebellious Archbishop Marcel LeFebvre, whose violent antipathy to Vatican II's updating of the church he shares, and whose activities he reportedly subsidizes.

Invitations to heads of Catholic agencies giving aid to Latin America were similarly selective. The German Adveniat and Misereor were reasonably included because of the extent of their aid, though one would have thought that after the strong protest of the German theologians Misereor hardly merited three representatives. Even stranger was the inclusion of Van Straaten's niece, Antonia Willemsen, aide to her uncle in Aid to the Suffering Church, while not inviting a single representative of various Dutch, Belgian, Spanish, Canadian, and other agencies that provide greater and more legitimate aid.

All these behind-the-scenes maneuvers were to give to the Puebla meeting a character significantly different from that of Medellin. It was only as the conference opened on January 28, 1979, having been postponed from October because of the death of Pope John Paul I, that it became publicly known that only the bishops—those elected and those nominated—would have votes. But the other appointed delegates had the right to speak.[1] Given the tight security and the isolation of the bishops in the Puebla seminary, the overall impact insured a highly conservative atmosphere and made it difficult to get to the attention of the many bishops, who had little understanding of the underlying issues, a balanced input of information from all viewpoints.

Progressive voices could not, however, be entirely excluded. Among those elected by their fellow bishops were Cándido Padin of Baurú, Brazil, the first to blow the whistle on the neofascist Doctrine of National Security; José Llaguno of Tarahumara, Chihuahua, Mexico, who is engaged in a long-term program to reconstruct pastoral work among the Indians by starting from their worldview; Leonidas Proaño of Riobamba, Ecuador, one who suffers constant persecution for his commit-

57

ment to the Indians who form the bulk of his parishioners, and with whom he proudly identifies as one of them; Oscar Romero of San Salvador, whose parting gift as he left for Puebla was a death warrant issued by a rightwing vigilante group; Dom Helder Camara and Cardinal Paulo Evaristo Arns, both of Brazil, two of the Latin American church's strongest voices for the voiceless, and various others.

Not all the progressive leaders were present. Notable among the missing were Pedro Casaldáliga, of São Felix, and Tomás Balduino of Goiás, both in the Amazon region now being opened up to destructive exploitation by Brazilian and global corporations, and both living in constant danger of death because of their defense of the Indians being dispossessed from their traditional homelands. Absent, too, was Miguel Obando of Managua, fearless in his denunciation of the tortures, disappearances, and murders being committed by the Somoza regime, Samuel Ruíz García of San Cristóbal, Mexico, Alberto Devoto of Goya, Argentina, and (in circumstances described earlier) Sergio Méndez Arceo of Cuernavaca, Mexico.

As mentioned briefly in the previous chapter, the Working Document that would constitute the official text designed to brief the delegates as to the specific purpose of the meeting was prepared by the CELAM secretariat in the deepest secrecy. Copies were printed only for those, including delegates, who had to read it, and each copy was marked so that the name of the person who had received it would show up on photocopies. The printers were sworn to absolute secrecy. Distribution was delayed until late September, so that even if copies did fall into hands of potential critics, they would not have time to prepare the kind of response that had greeted the PD. The script looked foolproof, but it didn't quite work.

First of all, page proofs were smuggled out of the printshop and 2,000 copies were on sale in Mexico City before the official edition was bound. This was quickly followed by a further edition of 1,000 copies in Brazil. Next, Pope John Paul I died in his sleep the night of September 28-29, forcing the postponement of the conference.

Much that went on behind the scenes, both before and after the death of John Paul I, is still far from clear. Writing in *Christianity and Crisis*, Harvey Cox and Faith Annette Sand say that "reputedly" Pope John Paul I, on the eve of his death, had bitterly fought with a curial cardinal who was trying to convince him to approve the lists of nominated delegates that had been so widely protested as one-sided. "The Pope had been so upset by the confrontation scene," they continue, "that some feel it caused his heart attack."

Some considerable light on what followed is shed by a letter written by López Trujillo some days after the election of John Paul II. Its authenticity was not challenged by López Trujillo, who wept with anger and vexation—according to eyewitnesses—when it was published in the Mexico City *Uno Más Uno* on 1 February 1979, just after the Puebla conference had opened. Reportedly, López Trujillo himself had given the tape cassette on which he had dictated it to a reporter in the belief that the tape was blank.

Addressed to Archbishop Luciano Cabral Duarte of Aracajú, Brazil (now first vice-president of CELAM), it opens by expressing the writer's satisfaction—"radiant with joy"—at the election of John Paul II. He comments: "As you see, he has begun to speak clearly." He next reports that he had a lot of trouble in having the Puebla meeting reconvoked for January, because some groups wanted an indefinite postponement or cancellation. What these people wanted was to leave things in a confused and ambiguous state, whereas López Trujillo sought to obtain from Puebla an "ideological platform" and "concrete and mature programs." This, he explained, was necessary as a preliminary to the upcoming election of new officers for CELAM, elections being "always dangerous."

Indicating that they had a fight on their hands, he urged Cabral Duarte to get ready for it. "Therefore, prepare your bombers, and also some of your sweet-tasting 'poison,' because you will need to be in top shape both for Puebla and for the CELAM elections. I think you should commit yourself to the kind of training boxers undertake before world championships. Let your smitings be evangelical and well-directed."

López Trujillo next describes his efforts to get the Brazilian bishops to curb Leonardo Boff, one of Brazil's top theologians. His latest book, he said, could not be more "confused and unpleasant." It actually proposes that lay persons "function as extraordinary ministers of the Eucharist without ordination."* "The sad part," López Trujillo continues, "is that the Congregation for Religious, faced with these and so many other deviations, goes on its way without the slightest eschatological tension.... All the tension it passes on to CELAM, giving us a headache with the unending pressures from CLAR."

The CLAR reference is to the long-standing conflict between López Trujillo and this body that represents the men and women religious of Latin America and is one of the major progressive church institutions in the hemisphere. The list of delegates issued by CELAM limited its representation at Puebla to its four top officers. Its protests to Rome brought instructions to CELAM to add sixteen further CLAR members. The letter of the order was obeyed but not the spirit. The sixteen chosen by the CLAR regions to represent them were rejected, and CELAM picked people more to its liking. The reference to the Congregation for Religious is to its head Cardinal Pironio who, as noted above, was conspicuously absent from the list. Protests to Rome succeeded in having him included, and similar protests caused Rome to add the name of

* Far from being confused, unpleasant or shocking, what Boff is said to propose is a widely established practice. Both authors of this book are, without ordination, extraordinary ministers of the Eucharist duly authorized by our bishop.

60

Jesuit General Arrupe. In his letter López Trujillo reveals his annoyance at this addition and suggests that Arrupe may complicate matters for him.

Obviously concerned to reduce the impact of the Brazilian progressives, López Trujillo hopes his friend has made contact with Cardinals Brandão Vilela and Sales, the two most conservative of Brazil's cardinals. "It seems to me," he adds, "that these two are going to Puebla with some optimism. And I believe, taking everything into account, that they have excellent reasons for their optimism." That he himself was optimistic is clear from the final paragraph of the letter which provides a mock-heroic touch. "Please write me. Let us work well, in close union with Cardinal Aponte [of San Juan, Puerto Rico, an ultraconservative]. With God's help the course of events will be positive. In any case, if they shoot me, do not fail to write an epitaph for me while you listen to records of Agustín Lara and read poems of Pablo Neruda. I offer a simple suggestion: 'He fought and he fell.' "

In this letter López Trujillo expressed his pleasure that he had succeeded in having the Puebla meeting rescheduled for January. Other reports just after John Paul II's election said he had tried to have it convened in November 1978 before the progressives, who lacked his financial resources, would have time to reorganize. With the delay to the end of January, they were able to study and publish their evaluations of the WD, and to arrange the massive presence and impact in Puebla (though outside the seminary) to be described shortly.

The WD marked a definite advance over the PD. Some of the bishops' conferences made severe criticisms and urged many changes and additions, some of these reflecting the input from the grassroots communities that had filtered through to the bishops. The WD properly identifies as the basic criterion the life and work of the church and the person of Jesus. It escapes from static or circular views of history, indicating a historical process: the moment of evil (the mystery of iniquity), the moment of being liberated from evil (the time of redemption), and the moment of attaining the positive goal (the time of reconciliation and communion). This dialectic process is illustrated by the history of Israel, and by the life, death, and resurrection of Jesus. But in applying this excellent concept to the reality of Latin America, the WD falters and fades away in generalizations. Its stress is on the final goal, unity and communion, ignoring what must precede it. Jesus did not preach a communion and unity as regards the conflicts between rich and poor. Unity and communion in Christ must be preceded by justice in history.

The WD's presentation of the sufferings of Jesus on the cross avoids analysis of the historic causes for these sufferings, thus running the risk of presenting the Father as the cause of his son's death. Underlying this ambiguity is the fear of offering a theology that would tend to disturb the status quo, since it would be forced to recognize that the cross of the poor is the cross of Jesus, that their despoliation and oppression are not willed by God but are the result of man's continuing sin.

The WD's treatment of the mystery of the church suffers from a like defect. The theological perspective is abstract and not rooted in history. Social and political structures are not looked at from the viewpoint of the poor, and in consequence the concrete tasks needed to build a human world are not seen as demanded by our Christian calling.

The end result is to distract attention from Latin America's central problem, namely, the injustice and violent exploitation and misery of millions of its inhabitants. Instead, the focus is secularism that is destroying the devout faith implanted during the colonial period. As explained earlier in this book, the assumption that the colonial age was a golden age of excellent evangelization is contrary to the facts. If secularism is destroying anything, it is the culturally dictated practices that are not supported by a living and lived faith. Also mistaken is the assumption of a single culture that has to be evangelized, when in fact Latin America has many cultures, the culture of the rich, the culture of the Spanish- or Portuguese-speaking poor, the culture of the Indians, and the ever-spreading culture of consumerism carried by the media of communications to the remotest areas from its North American home.

Finally, the transcendental importance of Medellin in the history of Christianity in Latin America did not come through in the WD. The history of contemporary persecution and martyrdom was ignored. The death of democracy was not linked to its cause, namely, a new phase of capitalist accumulation being paid for by the people in lowered living levels. Ecumenism was almost ignored. The role and rights of women were glossed over, and that in sexist language. It was indeed a far cry from the prophetic texts with which the bishops a decade earlier had started the task that culminated in the Medellin documents.

8. John Paul II Dramatizes Latin America's Dilemma

"Holy Father, see how the people admire you," President Ló-pez Portillo remarked to Pope John Paul II. "If I had only a fraction of such devotion, I would be in heaven."

This cordial conversation between the president of Mexi-co and the leader of the Roman Catholic Church took place in the privacy of the presidential palace on the occasion of the pope's historical visit to Mexico.

The reaction of the Mexican president puts in a nutshell the amazing impact the pope's visit had on Latin Americans and demonstrates the enormous value of popular feeling avail-able to the church to use in its task of evangelization to which the Puebla meeting was dedicated. And if this reverence for the pope survives so vigorously in Mexico in spite of genera-tions of anticlerical government, we can reasonably assume that the popular feeling is even stronger in other countries of Latin America.

Opposition to religion in Mexico is a carry over from a historic situation that no longer exists. The church has ceased to be a threat to the state. The hierarchical church cooperates with and legitimatizes the state. The state reciprocates by ig-noring violations of the Constitution and by making positive contributions, such as building the basilica at Guadalupe. While the laws remain on the statute books and in the Consti-tution, a *modus vivendi* has gradually been created so that the church and the state have learned to live together without feeling the need to change the laws. Legally, not only does the state own all the churches, but the priest lacks legal personality. He cannot vote, run for office, make a will, teach, inherit or wear the soutane in public. Yet Mexico has more priests in proportion to Catholics than any Latin American country except Colombia and Argentina. Effectively, all priests must be Mexicans, so Mexico is not dependent like those other countries on imports from Europe and North America. As in Poland, seminarians are plentiful. Government officials send their children to be taught by priests forbidden to teach in schools that officially do not exist. As the Mexicans say, relations are excellent between an illegal church and an excommunicated government.[1]

Although Poland gives the church far more leeway than most Communist countries, the church still insists that there are discriminations against believers because they are believers.[2] Freedom to publish books and periodicals, to broadcast, to build churches and name bishops without interference, the opportunity for Christians to earn jobs and degrees and educate their children in the faith without discrimination are limited. The regime is frightened that any concessions, even pragmatic, may create problems with its Soviet overlords. However, in recent years Party First Secretary Edward Gierek has gradually improved relations with the church, a policy that has strengthened his regime and the nation. The Kremlin reluctantly recognizes that the Polish government needs the support of the Catholic population.

The welcoming of the pope in Mexico involved a breach of the Constitution. President López Portillo had to walk the tight rope between official anticlericalism and the broad based political support of the church. The risk of offending the vast masses of Mexicans who came forth to express their affection and respect for the pope and through him the church was close.

The official position held by López Portillo presented him with another dilemma. Born into a staunch Spanish Catholic family, he had abandoned church practice which he found irrelevant as it functioned before Vatican II. Various well-informed people told us they believe that the cordial private welcome given by the president to the pope was an indication of his renewed interest in the conciliar church although his official position prevented him from expressing his changed attitudes publicly.

The pope and the president found ways of meeting their needs unofficially by the private visit to the president's home. Prior to John Paul's arrival, workmen were seen busy with some new construction and remodeling at the presidential palace. It was later learned that a special chapel was readied where the pope would celebrate Mass with the president's family.

Both the president and the pope were treading on delicate grounds. The pope was forced, by the logic of his stand, to ignore very concrete issues. For example, the condition of the people in Mexico contrasts unfavorably with that of the people in Poland. But if the pope were to make a big issue of the contrast, such confrontation would risk a rupture in the delicate relationships of church and state. In consequence, in contrast with the strong and specific statements made to the regime by John Paul on his recent visit to Poland (June 1979), he touched only in general terms on the conditions in Mexico and avoided any specific criticism of the government as causing or tolerating these conditions. Moreover, John Paul presumably realized that his knowledge of Latin America is far less complete than his knowledge of Poland, so that prudence dictated a cautious approach to the issues. His charge to the bishops at the opening of the Puebla meeting placed the onus on them as the people best equipped to apply general principles to concrete issues.

Why has Latin America fared differently from Poland?

Medellin, as we noted earlier, had singled out as the basic reason the control of the economy by domestic and foreign business interests. Mexico's daily *Excelsior* put the issue succinctly October 12, 1978. Four transnational corporations earn more money in Mexico (and export it) than the total income of the nation's agriculture, livestock and fisheries combined.[3]

No doubt some would try to hide the contrasts from John Paul as he crossed Mexico City from Guadalupe to Puebla. But how can anyone hide the reality of Netzahualcoyotl, the world's biggest cesspool into which Mexico has dumped two and a half million of the capital's more than 15 million inhabitants? It is not only the world's most populous slum, but the sights, sounds and smells of degradation exceed those one sees in Karachi, Calcutta, or the Philippines, as similar human vultures—men, women, children—circle the dumping grounds to snatch a piece of rotten meat or some scrap metal being unloaded from the trucks. And Netzahualcoyotl has its counterpart in every city of Latin America: in the *favelas* of Rio de Janeiro and São Paulo; in the *callampa* "Cuidad de Dios" in Lima; in the *barriada* "Veintiseis de Enero" in Santiago; in *barrio* "Lanus Oeste" in Buenos Aires; and in *villas miseria* in Santo Domingo, Caracas, Bogotá and elsewhere.[4]

Although John Paul has not seen these "situations of sin" with his own eyes, he has shown an appreciation of their meaning on various occasions since he became pope. "You have to call a spade a spade," he told the Vatican's Justice and Peace Commission (November 11, 1978). "We have to give the highest priority of attention to those who suffer from a total poverty, to those who suffer injustice. The church must seek models of development that call for sacrifice but without sacrificing the essential personal and social liberties and rights. And Christians must take the lead in developing ways of thinking and life styles that break decisively with the madness of the consumer society, a destructive and joyless society." Such words encouraged those who hoped that "the man from

67

far away" would take a firm stand with those who were following Medellin's call to liberate themselves from their dire oppression.

Another of the delicate factors John Paul had to take into account was the deep division within the Latin American hierarchy. From all the maneuvers and the countermaneuvers while Puebla was being prepared, it was obvious neither side would yield. John Paul had shown at different critical moments a willingness to temporize, a desire to avoid a direct confrontation. On one occasion, when he was archbishop of Krakow, he had gone to Rome and persuaded Paul VI to patch up a potentially serious split between Cardinal Wyszynski and Jerzy Turowicz of the Catholic publishing house *Znak*.[5] More recently, as pope, he had met the rebellious Archbishop Lefebvre without demanding a prior retraction. To ignore the division in Latin America, already an openly festering wound, could cause vastly greater harm to the people of Latin America, to the church's credibility, and to his own leadership.

Church leaders suffer from the human weakness of trying to hide their differences from the public, even from those they are called to serve and who have a strict right to know. The documents of Vatican II suffered in consequence; so did those of Medellin. To maintain a pretense of unity between irreconcilable theologies in today's desperate situation in Latin America would be a cruel deception. From all that has been said, it is clear that López Trujillo and his followers were betting on John Paul to use his authority to bring the progressive troops in line. Those leaders who had risked their lives in the struggle with the people for a decent human life could reasonably expect the Vicar of Christ to opt for the values lived and taught by Jesus. The world anxiously awaited the event that would reveal the person of John Paul II and his vision of the role of the church in these troubled times.

The stage was set. The characters were in place and thoroughly rehearsed. Mexico's bankers and tourist officials were frantically distributing props at airports, on streets, in churches. The world audience had been alerted by the electronic and printed media. All that was missing for curtain call was the arrival of the lead actor.

Clad in white soutane, passenger No. 68 on Alitalia flight 6566, listed under "H" of the alphabet for "Holy Father," John Paul II boarded the DC-10 without a ticket and without a passport. It was 8:30 Thursday morning, January 23, 1979, when the jetliner sailed into the air before the audience of world television. No small historic moment, this first international journey of Pope John Paul II—his first major initiative—would provide the world with the facts needed to project the path onto which this newly elected non-Roman pope would guide the Roman Catholic Church.

Destined for Puebla, Mexico, the pope chose a brief stopover in the Dominican Republic. This island holds the roots of Catholic evangelization in the Western hemisphere. Here was celebrated in 1494 the first Mass in the New World.

Upon arrival, and after a series of benedictions, midst rousing cheers, the new pope knelt to embrace and kiss the soil that had first received the Roman Catholic missionaries who accompanied Columbus on his second voyage. The adoration of throngs of people left no doubt among world viewers that the leader of the Roman Catholic Church holds an uncontested position of power.

Several of John Paul's personal attributes are readily observed. He is warm, charming, and self-confident. Only his Vatican aides were alarmed when, during the first hour of his flight, John Paul ventured into the cabin filled with news reporters and journalists for what resulted in an informal press conference. To one reporter who asked if he enjoyed being pope, he replied: "What is there to enjoy? It is a duty, and to do it I get a lot of help from Divine Grace and from the people." Those of us who followed him throughout his five-day trip, observing him to be always smiling, alert, nonchalant, concluded that he does indeed enjoy his new position, or else he possesses a more than average stage presence. When pressed regarding the most controversial issue of the Puebla conference, Liberation Theology, the pontiff was cautious: "Theology of liberation—yes. But one must be careful about applying doctrines of systems and ways of analysis which are not Christian . . ." He made it clear that socialism, when "not compatible with the Christian concept of man, of his rights, and with Christian morality" is not acceptable.

Some elements of the international press misconstrued this statement as a condemnation of Liberation Theology. However, analysis of the actual words of the pope both on this and on other occasions during his visit establishes quite clearly that while he warned against distortions of Liberation Theology, he did not condemn this theology. Indeed, after his return to Rome he made a strong statement insisting that liberation is an integral part of the Christian message.[6]

John Paul was specific in his insistence that it is the mission of the church to build "a more just, humane and livable world." In his emotionally charged homily to a crowd of more than 300,000 in the plaza of Santo Domingo he called on all Christians, bishops, priests, laity, to follow the example of Bartolomé de las Casas in the struggle. He addressed himself to those who live on the fringes, to the "landless peasants," to the "workers who are mistreated and given less than their full rights," and to "those unprotected by the law." He denounced the system which favors the "exploitation of man by man"— the "institutionalized corruption" that is sanctioned by the law of the powerful. This system, said the pope, allows "some to have too much while others lack everything"; in addition, "it permits children to be undernourished and uneducated."

While thousands from Latin America and elsewhere prepared for the long journey to Mexico to see their pope in person, those responsible for the big event busied themselves with readying Mexico for the occasion. Banners were strung across streets and hung from every window, saluting the pope as "The Pope from Poland," "Welcome, Holy Father," and petitioning "You who are holy, pray for us." Flags of the Vatican and of Mexico were reproduced in the millions and handed to the people to wave, to display on cars, from light poles. Placards bearing John Paul II's picture were distributed and displayed in store windows, in taxis and private cars, on billboards and traffic-light standards.

News correspondents and TV crews from around the world fought for space and special credentials to get nearest the pope. Some returned for the third and fourth day to obtain the card that had been applied for well in advance, being detained because the application had been misplaced, the right person was not in at the right time, more data required.

Last minute changes were made on the pope's agenda. Plans for a rally in the Azteca stadium were canceled because the entry tickets had been duplicated and widely distributed by some unknown source and it was feared that the crowd would be uncontrollable.

Mexico's president, López Portillo, ordered a three-day freeze on the sale of alcoholic beverages to insure order befitting his holiness.

In Mexico, as in the Dominican Republic, John Paul II's first public act was to kiss the soil. Millions swarmed the route from the airport to the Zócalo, the capital square, to catch a glimpse of "El Santo Papa." John Paul blessed and waved and blessed again the countless crowds who waved flags—yellow and white for the Vatican and red and green for Mexico— amid cheers of excitement and tears of joy. Never before had a pope set foot on their soil. No greater moment would happen in their lifetime. Weariness from the long wait in the blazing sun was quickly forgotten. "The pope has come to Mexico." One simple woman expressed her satisfaction by saying: "Jesus couldn't come himself, so he sent the pope."

Still blessing and gesturing to the crowd of more than three million, the pope descended from the open-air vehicle especially prepared for his tour and led the parade into the cathedral. He was escorted by the cardinals, bishops, monsignors, and lesser church officials, the order determined by their rank.

We left our lofty position atop the Majestic Hotel to find a television set where we could watch with the rest of the world the Mass that John Paul would celebrate and hear his first speech to the Mexican people and incidentally to the world.

Television cameras focused on a neatly arranged crowd of worshipers, nuns in this section according to the color of their uniforms, dignitaries here, and lay persons there. The Mass was a conventional Roman Catholic Eucharistic Liturgy. Missing was the mariachi music characteristic of Mexico's culture. In spite of the formalism of the situation, the person of the pope clearly affected everybody there. There was a sense of a unique moment and those who had the opportunity to participate were obviously moved by their feeling that they had become a part of history. Even one who had come to scoff later told us that he not only remained to pray but expressed his prayer in tears.

Recalling the loyalty of the Virgin, the pope appealed to the people to "strengthen this loyalty," and to translate it into "intelligence and a strong fidelity to the church of today." Referring to his words on his coronation day (October 22, 1978), he again asked for loyalty to the church of Vatican II. Quoting John XXIII, he spoke of the church as "rejuvenating and rediscovering itself"; as a servant of the world "because it makes the pleasures, hopes, and sorrows of the world its own." He summed up by reminding the people to be faithful to the Virgin, to the church, to the papacy, and to Christ.

Other major speeches were made by John Paul on the two

following days, again appearing cautious, theologically conservative, and warning against novelties. Later, in his talks with the Indians of Oaxaca and the industrial workers of Guadalajara, a major change of tone occurred. As in the Dominican Republic, the pope came out strongly in defense of the oppressed and developed the challenge to the unjust structures on which he had touched briefly in the third of his major addresses.

The second talk was at the shrine of the Virgin of Guadalupe, the spiritual center of Mexico. This event was the emotional high point of the pope's visit. An estimated five million people congregated in the blazing sun to cheer him. The sermon was one of intense and solid Marian piety, though strangely omitting the social content of the meaning of Guadalupe that Paul VI had stressed in two messages to the Mexican people. Instead, he pleased the conservatives by references that they read as a warning to slow down the drive for radical social change. He reaffirmed Medellin, saying it was "our point of departure." He continued, saying that some had "given it interpretations at times contradictory, not always correct, not always beneficial for the church." Since he did not specify where the line should be drawn, conflict was compounded rather than resolved.

At the Palafoxian Seminary at Puebla, the scenario was reenacted. In costumes that reflected every state and region of Mexico, the vast crowds waited patiently under the blazing sun to greet their sainted leader. A priest at the microphone thundered across the open grounds the greatness and the virtues of the holy one who was about to come. At intervals, this rousing cheerleader would rehearse slogans: "Rah, rah, rah! . . . Viva Polonia! . . . Viva Wojytla! . . . Rah, rah, rah!"

"Here is Jesus Christ in the person of the pope," the clerical cheerleader finally announced. As John Paul appeared on the platform forty to fifty feet above their heads, the people cheered and shrieked until their voices grew hoarse. Tears filled many eyes fastened on the tiny white figure atop the platform—tiny because so far away.

The two papal talks in Puebla, one to the public at the open-air Eucharist, the second to the conference delegates, amplified the themes of the previous days. There were very positive elements. Medellin should be the starting point for Puebla. The bishops must not ignore the challenges to human dignity in the hemisphere. Paul VI's condemnation of "mechanisms" [structures] that on the international level increase the wealth of the rich at the expense of increasing the poverty of the poor was recalled, as was Paul VI's identification of human rights with commitment to the most needy. Medellin's preferential option for the poor was specifically reaffirmed. Also important was the mention of the "social mortgage" that affects ownership and use of property. This is indeed traditional church doctrine as formulated by Thomas Aquinas and others, but has tended to be overlooked by the stress on the rights of private property in recent centuries.[7] This official church teaching points clearly and specifically to the obligation to use property for the benefit of society. John Paul gave the theological foundation to be applied concretely to the Latin American reality. It would mean that a corporation making profit is obliged to use the profit to insure living wages for workers. The living reality of the rich and poor in Latin America documents the fact that the social mortgage teaching has not been taken to heart.

Other elements were less helpful. It was refreshing to find a recognition of the primacy of Jesus Christ in the life of the Christian after an earlier speech had formulated the priorities as fidelity to the church, to the pope, to Mary, and to Jesus. The point would have been stronger were it not for a context that prepared the way for rejection of the serious efforts of many recent European theologians and some Latin American liberation theologians to develop a Christology compatible with the conclusions of contemporary biblical exegesis and the contributions of the life sciences.

The importance of this issue cannot be exaggerated, according to Jon Sobrino, S. J.[8] The newer theologians take the historical Jesus as their starting point: "the person, teachings, attitudes, and deeds of Jesus of Nazareth insofar as they are accessible, in a more or less general way, to historical and exegetical investigation" (p. 3). They do so because they believe that if a Christology disregards the historical Jesus, it turns into an abstract theology that is historically alienating and open to manipulation. (Alienating because it has nothing to do with the real life of Christians today; open to manipulation because it can be used to reinforce patterns of political and ecclesiastical domination.)

The concerns of López Trujillo and of the PD and WD were strongly reflected. John Paul deplored "incorrect interpretations of Medellin," "ideologies," and "rereadings of the gospel." He noted an attitude of mistrust "with regard to the institutional church or official church," rejected the possibility of a "parallel magisterium," insisting that "everyone has the duty to avoid magisteria other than the church's magisterium."

What came across was a strong resistance to theological pluralism, an insistence that the pope and bishops are the *maestros*—a word that in Spanish carries the overtones of proprietor and instructor—of a truth fixed for all time. The function of the faithful is reduced to accepting and obeying that truth.

Protestants who had come to Puebla with high hopes that the pope, who in Poland had stood up firmly against state aggression, would be equally strong in opposition to Latin America's neofascist dictatorships, were disillusioned by anti-ecumenical overtones in his addresses, and by the blessing of a "religiosity" that interposes the church and the Virgin as mediators between the saving Christ and his brothers and sisters. Encouragement of this tradition retards the evolution of Latin

American Catholicism into an intellectually based religion meaningful to all Christians.

At Oaxaca he delivered a ringing condemnation of poverty and expressed his full support of the demands of the Indians to have their lands restored to them. "This pope wants to identify with the cause of the humble and the poor. He is with the masses who are nearly always abandoned at an ignominious living level and at times harshly exploited. . . . He wants to be your voice, the voice of those who cannot speak because they are muzzled. . . . Workers must not be forced to wait longer for full recognition of their equal dignity. They have the right to demand that barriers of exploitation raised by selfish people with the power to hold them down be stripped away. They are entitled to adequate aid that is not a handout or a few crumbs of justice so that they can achieve the development they merit as human beings and children of God." Similarly at Guadalajara, he urged the industrial workers—as he had frequently done in Poland—to stand up for their rights.

We may have to wait a generation or a century for a definitive judgment on the significance of John Paul's visit to the New World. Some points, however, can be underscored. Perhaps the clearest is that the important actors were the pope and the people. In the final quarter of the twentieth century, a materialist and skeptical world witnessed the magnetic appeal the head of the Roman Catholic Church still holds over the millions who poured into the streets—and the countless millions glued to television screens—to testify with their feet, their voices, their ecstasy to their allegiance. This reality, repeated more recently in Poland, no government can with impunity ignore. Obviously, the Mexican government saw the obvious, and other Latin American governments must be more aware than ever before of the extraordinary potential the church still enjoys.

What is less clear is whether the pope and the bishops have the skills and the unity needed to channel this potential in ways that will benefit not only the institution but the material and spiritual renewal of the society. Sergio Torres, a Chilean priest who is executive secretary of Theology in the Americas in New York and who worked with other liberation theologians at Puebla, has commented as follows: "The pope faced a great challenge in coming to Latin America. He had to combine the particularity of his personal experience in Poland with his ministry to the universal church. It is not a lack of respect to say that the pope has to learn to be a pastor of the universal church. The gift of the Spirit in his role does not exclude the painful process of learning and assimilating the experience of other churches. The particular experience of the Polish church cannot be transferred or applied to other countries and continents."[9]

It is also important to note that the pope during his visit communicated in different ways. The formal addresses were possibly less important than his behavior, his attitudes, his obvious love, his concern for the poor, his friendly manner with children. All of this nonverbal projection placed the bishops in a stronger position to make their decisions at the conference without being concerned about who might be pleased or displeased, especially as John Paul made amply clear that he was not telling them what to do. How they responded will emerge in the following chapters.

9. Dialogue Through Bars

Cardinal Lorscheider, President of CELAM, on the first working day of the conference set a very positive tone for the meeting. "Isn't it possible," he said, "for the institutional church not to look so much at itself in regard to functioning better and for it to occupy itself a little more with the world of men?" It soon became clear that if Puebla was going to concern itself more with the "world of men" and less with itself, it would not be in the sight of men—or women!

After hustling for taxis to get to Palafoxian Seminary to get their big stories, the reporters discovered a wall constructed to cut the bishops off from the press. This wall was described by Bishop Dario Castrillón, Communications Department president, as "the wall of liberty." His assumption was that by isolating themselves from the church and the world, the bishops would be freer to evaluate the world and the church.

The organization of the conference was quite different from that of Medellin. At Medellin, the delegates were allowed several days for free discussion, dialogue and sharing. This format provided the opportunity for bishops coming from all parts of Latin America to get to know one another better as they shared their personal histories and life experience relative to the way each viewed his role or function in the church. Later in the conference, when issues were debated and decisions made, those voting had an advantage of a broader perspective concerning the needs of the church in the hemisphere.

At Puebla, the 350 delegates were immediately divided into twenty-one working groups, each instructed to study a section of the WD with freedom to approve, to modify, or to reject entirely and produce a new proposal. After two days, each commission would submit an interim report to the Coordinating Commission for examination regarding overlapping, contradictions, or omissions. These reports would then be shared with all delegates so each group could return to a second working period with knowledge of what the others were doing. Revised reports returned to the Coordinating Commission for collation and a presentation of the document or documents for discussion and approval.

Bishop Leonidas Proaño (Riobamba), a major spokesman for the progressives, described the five members named to the Coordinating Commission as "people in whom we have confidence." They were: Bishop Marcos McGrath (Panama), Chairman; Juan Flores (La Vega, Dominican Republic); Luciano Mendez (Auxiliary, São Paulo, Brazil); Luis Bambaren (Chimbote, Peru); and Justo Laguna (San Isidro, Argentina).

The delegates were free to choose their commission. Curia representatives and other conservatives spread themselves strategically throughout the major working groups. Not all were happy with this arrangement. As Cardinal Lorscheider said with a smile at a press conference, "It is not easy to confront a Curia cardinal."

Medellin broke protocol by issuing its decisions on its own authority without first submitting them to Rome. Puebla issued its conclusions, but made clear that they were provisional until Rome studied and perhaps rewrote. In fact, the final version did include changes made by Rome.

The journalists quickly recognized that those who controlled the machinery of the conference were determined to keep them as confused and as ignorant as possible about what was or was not happening. They continued to compete for taxis during the early morning rush hour to be the first to receive the daily "official press release," always with too few copies and generally in Spanish only. The bulletin contained brief references to the order of the previous day, with such details as who presided over the liturgy with which each morning session was convened, what scripture was read, and some remarks made by the homilist. Following would be a progress report on the commissions without substantive content.

The official press conferences were highly managed. Questions had to be submitted in advance, thus allowing time to prepare answers. The process of selection of the bishops who would answer questions was never revealed. Long wordy answers were read from carefully prepared scripts. There was no discussion, impromptu questions, or exchange between the journalists and the answering panel members. The least threatening questions were taken first and time was fixed so that the more challenging issues were never reached. One reporter told of repeating the process of presenting her question eight days in succession to no avail.

Such manipulation of the press was a short-sighted policy on the part of the organizers of Puebla. By antagonizing the press, by hiding facts and giving half truths, they guaranteed that the world view of Puebla would be distorted and seen through hostile eyes, when in fact most of the press people came full of hope and desire to see the church becoming a more significant part of the solutions for the world's problems. Their frustration was heightened because of their inability to believe that a major institution in the twentieth century could have such a distorted understanding of the press and the function of public relations.

Not satisfied with the "tid-bits" of meaningless information that came through the official channels, the well-seasoned journalists began to look for other resources. It was easy to track the pattern of some bishops who habitually arrived early and departed late. Reporters began to chase after those they wanted to interview as they came and went through the entrance corridor leading to the separating wall. Dozens would surround a delegate, armed with tape recorders and cameras, shouting questions above the rumble, and jotting down every word that was audible. Probably every statement uttered in that crowded hallway found its way to print in several different languages, and as many variations of content.[1]

Requests to interview particular delegates could be made in writing. These appointments would be scheduled at a given time and place, the results being posted on a special bulletin board arranged for the purpose. By the end of the first day, the board was filled with regrets marked in red ink that the work of the conference was too demanding to allow time for the interview. The special bulletin board stretched along the corridor wall filled with "regrets" was aptly renamed the "wall of misinformation."

As resistance to press manipulation grew, the journalists became more aggressive. They began to hiss and boo when panel members avoided issues. Two confrontations were staged in support of five colleagues denied accreditation. This was followed by a strong statement charging the bishops with violation of the church's own rules, most recently restated by John Paul II in his address to journalists in Rome, October 13, 1978. "Church institutions should receive with respect for their convictions and their profession those who report religious news, providing them with documentation that is both fully adequate and absolutely objective." The bishops' failure to do this, the statement said, is a violation of the inalienable right to information.

The opportunity was also lost to evangelize the press, a priority in evangelization because of the multiplier effect. Regrettably, the gap between bishops and press was now so wide that the only response to the protest was a lecture from the press panel about irresponsible reporting.

Despite all this, reporters were encouraged by reliable sources such as Bishop Proaño that "the atmosphere at the meeting is daily more brotherly, more friendly, more optimistic." One reason for this was suggested by John William Saelman, a Dutch Augustinian provincial, who represented the Dutch bishops, invited because of their major aid-giving activities. According to Saelman, many bishops were not equipped, not prepared, not interested in making statements about doctrine. Their concerns were local—how to get from Puebla what would help each in running his diocese and what would take the pressures off him. Seeing the shortage of priests as the principal problem, they kept asking the European and North Americans present for more priests. They were unable to envision any alternatives, whether more vocations, the recruitment of lay ministers, or the possibility of married or women priests.

A few of the observers at the conference offered their services to the press. One of these was Bishop Thomas C. Kelly, secretary general of the U.S. Catholic Conference. He responded openly to questions from large groups of English speaking reporters. He spoke of being moved by the pope's visit, and by the brotherly spirit among the bishops at the meeting, despite their theological differences. He was optimistic regarding the impact the Puebla meeting would have on the church in the U.S. Current press coverage has noted that both he and Archbishop John R. Quinn, president of the U.S. Catholic Conference of Bishops, have made strong statements concerning the intense suffering that Nicaraguans, especially the poor, are experiencing. Archbishop Quinn was reportedly so impressed by the Puebla conference that he is anticipating a similiar meeting of the North American bishops.

Outside the walls of Palafoxian Seminary where the self-incarcerated bishops held their cloistered meeting, there took place a truly ecclesial event—priests, nuns, lay persons, joined by some of the conference bishops and by bishops who were not chosen to participate—celebrating life in all its dimensions. Very many concerned groups seized the opportunity to caucus at Puebla, simultaneously with the bishops' meeting. They recognized that they had here a "political forum" not only in the limited sense of reaching some of the bishops but in the broader sense of taking advantage of the publicity being generated and distributed worldwide by printed and electronic media. The refusal of most bishops to cooperate with the press was for these concerned groups a bonus. The journalists needed news and they were happy to oblige. Because the conditions, the issues, the problems that rape Latin America are global both in their causes and in their consequences, it was extremely important to develop world awareness and concern.

Argentine women came to ask John Paul's help in locating their 14,000 relatives, disappeared since 1976. Being restrained by the ruthlessly effective security personnel—reportedly recruited from neofascist organizations—they waited outside the great steel doors that breached the three-meter fence surrounding the Puebla seminary. Relentlessly but unsuccessfully they challenged the bishops to include in their program of "evangelizing Latin America" a specific condemnation of the institutionalized violence in their homeland.

Joining the Argentines were mothers from El Salvador and Nicaragua, coming "in spite of our pain." We expect, they said, that "the church, more than politicians, should assume the defense of human rights and give this priority."

Priest, poet and guerrilla leader Ernesto Cardenal, accompanied the Nicaraguans in a "liturgical" celebration using poetry, film, and music, to retell the horror they had experienced at the hand of the Somoza dictatorship.[2] They viewed the work of the bishops as "a critical moment to denounce the genocide to which the Nicaraguan people are subject."

Enlightened Haitians, silenced by the government with the support of the institutional church, were supported by contingents living in exile in Canada and New York. They denounced the bishops (all named by the government under a

83

Concordat signed in 1860) who express publicly their support of the regime, "using their sermons to reinforce old dogmas of respect for authority and resignation to the injustice of this earthly life."

A statement signed by 53 base groups of Guatemala protested recent massacres of peasants, and their wives and children, by big landholders supported by motorized police units. "We want you," they told the bishops, "to reaffirm the recent insistence of the Synod of Bishops that the church has the duty to condemn situations of injustice when basic human rights are involved."

Representatives of twenty million Hispanics from the United States called upon the bishops to acknowledge the "racism and discrimination" evidenced by the fact that of 350 U.S. bishops, only nine are Hispanic. They condemned the injustices perpetrated against the millions of undocumented aliens. The Chicanos among them added that they seek a pastor, are frustrated and crushed by an inability to understand the function of the church in the United States Southwest.

Medellin had earlier dwelt on a theme that constantly recurred in the messages of the *comunidades de base* to Puebla and in the statements of the liberation theologians, namely, the overwhelmingly negative impact of United States international policies and the practices of the U.S.-based global corporations on Latin America. The situation was further highlighted during the conference when a major Mexico City newspaper featured a report that President Carter had ordered the CIA to gather "more and better information about the churches in Latin America."

This report, coupled with the announced visit to Mexico of President Carter immediately after the conference to look for oil and gas and try to make some deal to ease border conflict caused by the growing number of undocumented Mexicans coming north in search of work, prompted more than a hundred North Americans to hold a press conference under

CENCOS auspices. Out of this came a letter to President Carter signed by Felipe Berryman, Mary Buckley, Betty Campbell, Harvey Cox, Robert Kennedy, Dow Kirkpatrick, Mary O'Keefe, Robert Pelton, Rosemary Ruether, Faith Sand, Paul David Sholin, Helen Volkmener, and many other North Americans known for their inter-American concerns.

Protesting yet another CIA offensive against church people in Latin America who identify with the poor, when the real problems are internationally sponsored and supported policies that mean "fewer jobs, lowered real wages, more hunger, fewer social services," it urged President Carter to come to see the Latin America they know. It condemned his manipulation of "human rights," ignoring the right of the poor: "the social rights to life, land, work, food, clothing, housing, education, economic security, health, and personal dignity."

As specific steps, the writers urged Carter to renounce publicly as unnecessary and inappropriate CIA penetration and infiltration of the church in Latin America. They called for an end of support to and severance of diplomatic relations with the repressive Somoza regime "established and maintained by the United States since the 1930s." They warned against pressures on Mexico during the upcoming visit to cede its "unrenewable natural resources too rapidly with little benefit for the Mexican people." They reaffirmed the pleas of the Spanish-speaking North Americans to end "the duplicity of United States immigration policy" and to enact legislation that would respect the rights of all.

Finally, they warned that the harvest of injustice we have sown abroad is coming home to be reaped, asserting that the "national security states" established under our tutelage are increasingly eroding what we regard as essential freedoms in the United States, for example, extensive surveillance of private citizens. "Should we be surprised that many people around the world, experiencing United States policies, come to see the United States as the 'enemy'? It seems to us that we need a basic change in direction so that United States policies need not be maintained by force and control only."

Women, too, came from all over North and South America to assert their existence. Called *Mujeres para el Diálogo* (Women for Dialogue), they identified themselves as a movement rather than a group, operating without an internal hierarchy, democratically making decisions with the aid of a nucleus to help communication and cooperation. The forums held in Puebla were initiated by Betsy Hollants, founder of CIDHAL, a research center on women in Latin American society, based in Cuernavaca, Mexico. Assisting Betsy in directing the conference were Rosemary Ruether, U. S. Roman Catholic historian and theologian, a pioneer in the movement for total liberation of women; Victoria Reyes from Peru, whose primary concern is domestic help; Ada Maria Isasi-Diaz, coordinator of the U.S. Women's Ordination Conference; and theologian Yolanda Lallande, who performs all the ministries other than eucharistic in a parish in Cuernavaca, Mexico.

The women came well prepared. Position papers were distributed to the press, to liberation theologians, and to the bishops.[3] These dealt with "human and liberation theology," "theology of religious life," "woman as the key to liberation," "the family in our society," "status of domestic help in Latin America," "ministering women in grassroots communities," and many other pertinent issues. Martha Sanchez Gonzalez of Mexico gave an excellent analysis of family planning. While warning of the threat to freedom hidden in many programs, she insisted on the possibility of a "just and liberating use" of such planning in the proper social context, thus ending one of the major oppressions of women.

The religious women were particularly vocal. They described themselves as "used by the church to maintain a structure of domination." They lamented the image of "a church without women" transmitted to the world via television covering the triumphal visit of John Paul II. Even more, they lamented the majority of religious and laywomen who do not even know that they are oppressed; who humbly accept their role as "protector of life."

It is doubtful that these women, conscious of the mandate to the church to enflesh the gospel in the world, yearned to be elevated to one of the formidable positions on the hierarchical pyramid of pope and male clerics that posed symbolically and actively on the podium high above the people at Palafoxian Seminary to open the CELAM conference. Specifically, the "Women for Dialogue" rejected the existing cultic priesthood that is "clerical, hierarchic, racist, and classist." They sought equal participation in a priesthood "discerned as a gift of the Spirit through the community in which it lives and works, and accepted and validated by the universal church through the bishops."

The women failed in their attempts to obtain a caucus with the bishops and other official delegates, especially the women delegates. They did establish some meaningful relationships with progressive bishops and other individuals, using these as liaison to get their message to the attention of the conference. This work had positive concrete results. Although the final statement falls short of their position, it does incorporate several elements that were lacking in the earlier draft. Enrique Dussel noted that the Puebla document contains the first reference to women in an official church statement in the history of Latin America.

Interacting closely with these special-interest groups were some of the world's best theologians and social scientists, the protagonists of Liberation Theology. They included: Gustavo Gutierrez, Leonardo and Clotildo Boff, Enrique Dussel, Hugo Assman, Pablo Richard, Raul Vidales, Jon Sobrino, Luis del Valle, José Comblin, and others. They did not come to manipulate or to set up a parallel conference, still less a counter-conference. Many were invited by their respective bishops and they did in fact make important contributions by evaluating drafts for sympathetic bishops. They lived as they could, met where they could, in convents, in small hotels, in private homes. In "unofficial press conferences," they affirmed their solidarity with those who were pleading for the imprisoned without trial, those in torture chambers, the exiles, the parentless children, the rights of the millions of undocumented in the United States. They were not afraid to speak, even though they made no claim to be "maestros" of the truth. All they could tell was their own experience and the experiences of their people.

The journalists fought their way into the halls in which the periti spoke, knowing that these were the people best qualified to analyze the reality of Latin America. Comblin commented to us that it was we (the journalists) and not the bishops who would tell the world the meaning of the Puebla event.

Gustavo Gutierrez spoke not to defend Liberation Theology but on behalf of the poor, the marginalized and the despoiled, claiming that all "self-identified" Christians will stand with them, letting the Jesus message they reveal drive us to action to achieve complete liberation for all.

Xabier Gorostiaga, a Panama Jesuit economist, outlined economic and political factors as a framework for evaluating the Latin American church, thus offering a reason to question papal and episcopal injunctions against political involvement. Agreeing with the pope that the Christian's goal is not political, Gorostiaga pointed out that "so long as structures of violence exist in Latin America, the church must speak and act against them."

At the conclusion of the final public Mass, the Puebla Document was symbolically presented to each of the presiding prelates of the twenty-two attending nations. In the next chapter we shall see what it offered as a blueprint for the next decade, and the extent to which it fulfilled or dashed the conflicting hopes of the many who had sought to influence its spirit and thrust.

10. The Bishops Take Their Stand

As was perhaps inevitable, the document put together by more than twenty distinct working groups in a couple of weeks is far from being fully integrated. It has gaps, duplications, a variety of emphases, not a few contradictions. It seldom sings. It seldom prophesies. Aware of the reality of the profound divisions within the assembly, yet also pressed by Pope John Paul to maintain a united front, the drafters hesitated to express their own thoughts, searching in earlier church statements—especially in the addresses of John Paul II—for safe formulations. Such an approach produces much chaff, which one has to winnow to find the grain.

There is, however, some real grain for those prepared to search. The formulation of the basic function and duty of the church, the specific theme of the meeting, is unexceptionable. Evangelization is presented in the same spirit as is found in the account in Saint Matthew of Jesus' reply to the disciples of John the Baptizer, when he said, "Go and tell John what you hear and see: the blind receive their sight and the lame walk, lepers are cleansed and the deaf hear, and the dead are raised up, and the poor have the good news proclaimed to them." It is no empty promise that Jesus gave or that the church must give. Proclaiming the good news is its efficacious application to healing the injustices that are the fruit of sin.

Here are some of the ways in which the Puebla Final

Document (FD) formulates its preferential option for the poor. "The Third Latin American Episcopal Conference reaffirms, with renewed hope in the life-giving power of the Spirit, the position of the Second General Conference [Medellin] which made a clear and prophetic option of preference for and identification with the poor" (FD Par. 1134). "The commitment to the poor and oppressed and the development of the grassroots communities have helped the church to discover the evangelizing power of the poor, to the extent that they constantly challenge the church, calling it to be converted, and to the extent that they express in their own lives the evangelical virtues of mutual support, service, simplicity, and readiness to grasp God's gift" (FD Par. 1147). "By drawing close to the poor in order to walk with them and serve them, we do what Christ taught us when he made himself our brother, poor like us. For this reason, service to the poor is the privileged means, though not to the exclusion of other means, for us to follow Christ. The best service to our brother is evangelization that makes him ready to fulfill his potential as a child of God, frees him from injustices and develops him as a full human being" (FD Par. 1145).

In consequence, "the evangelical commitment of the church, as the pope said, must be like that of Christ: a commitment to the most needy" (FD Par. 1141). But in order to be effective, "it is supremely important that this service to the brother be in the line established by Vatican Council II (Decree on Laity, Par. 8): 'The demands of justice should first be satisfied, lest the giving of what is due in justice be represented as the offering of a charitable gift. Not only the effects but also the causes of various ills must be removed. Help should be given in such a way that the recipients may gradually be freed from dependence on others and become self-sufficient' " (FD Par. 1146). An indispensable preparatory step for the church if it is to live and proclaim the need for Christian poverty, is "to revise its structures and the life of its members, especially its

91

pastoral agents, with a view to a meaningful conversion" (FD Par. 1157).

This paragraph, though still forceful, is one of many in which revision in Rome toned down the text voted at Puebla. The Rome revision dropped the following sentence, which read: "When the church is thus converted, it will be able to evangelize the poor effectively." There is nothing novel about this concept of the church needing continual conversion. It was sanctified by Saint Augustine.[1]

According to the Rome weekly *NTC News*, whose information about what goes on inside the Roman Curia is most reliable, López Trujillo spent several weeks in Rome "correcting" the Puebla Document.[2] The many changes introduced significantly alter the text voted by the bishops. Some changes are legitimately editorial, adjusting the order of words to clarify what was the obvious intention. Some are arbitrarily editorial, substituting one synonym or grammatical construction for another. But there are many significant changes of substance, like the one just indicated, and their overall purpose is clear. In the spirit of the writings of Roger Vekemans, each modification is designed to weaken or challenge the position of the liberation theologians. Some go further, seeking to restore the monopoly enjoyed for a century or more by the so-called Roman School of Theology, a monopoly breached only when Vatican II reasserted the legitimacy of theological pluralism as it had existed from the earliest times and had flourished most notably in the golden age of Scholasticism.

Shortly after the Revised Document (RD) was released, Mexican bishop Samuel Ruiz said basic changes had been made in the FD, offering as a specific example the modification of Puebla's condemnation of the Doctrine of National Security. Puebla had made the condemnation absolute, but the RD makes it only conditional. A colleague, Bishop Rafael García Ramírez, said the Mexican bishops' conference should ask the Vatican why the changes had been made.

92

The "anguish" of the people in the FD is softened in the RD to their "suffering." The word "vital" replaces "liberating." When "economic crisis" is discussed, an added phrase states that this crisis is occurring "in spite of the trend to modernization, with vigorous economic growth"; this without also noting that the claimed economic growth, seldom vigorous, is making the rich richer and the poor poorer.

A particularly revealing omission occurs when the FD speaks of the "hierarchical ministry" confided by Jesus to the church. It is a quite conventional statement: "This ministry was confided to Peter and the Twelve, whose successors today are the Roman Pontiff and the bishops, to whom are joined as co-workers the priests and deacons. *It is a ministry intended to be exercised collegially, since it is a participation in a single ministry.* The pastors of the church do not merely guide it in the name of the Lord. They further exercise the function of masters of the truth and preside sacerdotally over divine worship . . ." (FD #158). In the RD (#259) the phrase in italics is simply omitted.

Considerable confusion results from a lack of clarity about the meaning of ideology.[3] Every individual and every society has an ideology. It is the theoretical and analytical structure of thought that undergirds successful action either to realize revolutionary change in society or to undergird and justify the status quo. Its usefulness is proved in the success of its practices. Its validity is that it expresses the self-understanding, the hopes and values of the social group that holds it, and that it guides the practice of that group. The concrete issue is whether a particular ideology reflects a bias or social illusion, or whether it reflects truth or social insight. At one point the FD seems to grasp this distinction, but frequently it rejects a viewpoint it disapproves by dismissing it as an ideology, without clarifying whether the particular view is a social illusion or a social insight.

The method by which the FD was prepared in a series of

93

separate groups, with inadequate coordination (as explained earlier), understandably produced some elements that were better than others. The eighteenth commission's statement on "Preferential Action for the Poor," some extracts from which have already been quoted, is by far the best. Its fifteen members included three religious sisters from Cuba, Panama, and the Dominican Republic; three laymen from Brazil and Paraguay; nobody from the Roman Curia. It stressed the church's need for profound conversion, recognized (in open conflict with claim made elsewhere in the Puebla documents) that the church in Latin America is deeply divided, and admitted that "we must confess that not all of us who hold positions of responsibility in the Latin-American church have identified fully with the poor and that we do not always present the image of an evangelically poor church." Existing church structures and attitudes make it difficult to permit the church to live the Christian poverty that is required for the accomplishment of its missions, and in consequence "a genuine conversion of all sectors of the church to a full identification with a poor Christ, incarnated in the poor, is essential."

The commission also rejected the claim made in the Secretariat's WD that poverty is not exclusively a privation and marginalization from which we must liberate ourselves, but also a positive life style that "flourished in the Old Testament." Presumably it feared that such a distinction could be used by the rich to justify a continuation of the grossly unequal distribution of goods and services characteristic of Latin-American economies.

The Rome revision toned down somewhat the enthusiasm of the eighteenth commission. In addition to softening the call to the church to be converted, it showed a hesitancy about ecumenical cooperation by omitting Puebla's appeal to join forces with other churches in a common struggle to root out poverty and build a better world. But all in all, this remains Puebla's best effort.

Compared with Medellin, however, little new emerges. Medellin had already made clear that poverty expresses solidarity with the oppressed and a protest against oppression. It called on the church to implement this poverty by evangelizing the poor, denouncing injustice, establishing a simple life style for all its leaders, a spirit of service, freedom from temporal ties, intrigue, or ambitious prestige.[4] In its *Conclusions*, it had asserted clearly that the image projected by the Latin-American church was not that of a poor church. And it also distinguished clearly the three meanings of poverty. "Poverty, as a lack of the goods of this world necessary to live worthily as humans, is in itself evil. The Prophets denounce it as contrary to the will of the Lord and most of the time as the fruit of the injustice and sin of men. . . . The one who is spiritally poor values the goods of this world but does not become attached to them, recognizing the higher values of the riches of the kingdom. . . . The one who makes a voluntary commitment to poverty and lovingly assumes the conditions of the needy in order to bear witness to the evil it represents follows the example of Christ who took to himself all the consequences of our sinful condition. . . . In this context, a poor church denounces the unjust lack of this world's goods and the sin that begets it; preaches and lives in spiritual poverty, as an attitude of spiritual childhood and openness to the Lord; is bound to material poverty. The poverty of the church is, in effect, a constant factor in the history of salvation."[5]

By contrast with Puebla's statement on poverty, the Document on the Laity is essentially preconciliar. The commission that prepared it was headed by an Italian bishop, a member of the Roman Curia. More than half the church is discarded with a passing reference to women as co-responsible with men in the construction of the new civilization. The main thrust is in favor of "Catholic Action" organizations, stressing Pope Pius XI's concept of the laity as foot-soldiers carrying out unquestioningly the orders of the higher officers. All of this is light-years away from the self-understanding long since acquired by the Latin-American grassroots communities, as explained earlier.

What is said in the statement on the laity has to be correlated with the roles assigned to clergy and laity in the statement on ideologies and politics as they relate to evangelization. Here we have a clear withdrawal from the thinking both of Vatican II and of Medellin. The thrust of these ecclesial gatherings was that the clergy had the right and duty to work side by side with the laity to struggle against oppression and help build the kind of society God had intended as the goal of his creation. Puebla takes a different view. Bishops and priests are defined as the "ministers of unity in the church." As such it pertains to them to deal with politics "in the wider and superior sense,... the common good,... fundamental community values,... interior concordance and exterior security," and similar ethereal matters.

These "ministers of unity," however, are directed by Puebla to resist the temptation to mix "the things of God with merely political attitudes." That is "party politics" and is "the proper sphere of the layperson." Party politics is clearly defined. It includes the activity of groups of citizens whose objective is to obtain and exercise political power to resolve economic, political, and social issues according to their particular criteria and ideologies. The ideologies developed by these groups, even when inspired by Christian teachings, can reach different conclusions. In consequence, no political party, no matter how deeply inspired by the church's teachings, has the right to reserve to itself the representation of all the faithful, because its concrete program can never have absolute value for all.

Superficially, this formulation would seem unexceptionable. But on closer examination, it will be seen to deal with situations that have no pertinence to the reality of contemporary Latin America. It assumes that the citizens are free to organize, to formulate their platforms, to propose different solutions to problems on the nature of which the society has a consensus. It assumes a reasonably stable equilibrium in the division of power among the major groups in the society. In such a context it would be legitimate to quote, as the Puebla Document does the statement in Vatican II's Constitution on the Church in the Modern World: "Secular duties and activities belong properly *although not exclusively* to the laity"; although it would not be a fair quotation to omit, as both the Puebla Document and the Rome revision do, the words in italics.

The situation confronting the people of Latin America and the church is radically different. Almost everywhere, as the Puebla Document elsewhere recognizes and the Medellin documents had already stated even more vigorously, the most elementary human rights are being trampled upon. Political parties, trade unions and other groups intermediate between the citizen and the state are destroyed or domesticated. Powerful individuals, often with private armies and always claiming they are acting in the name of religion, drive peasants and Indians off the land they have cultivated from time immemorial, burning homes and crops, imprisoning, torturing and killing those who try to defend their livelihood and their families. The issues are economic, political, and social; and as such, Puebla says they are the exclusive concern of the laity. Even with the leadership of committed bishops, priests, and religious, many of whom in the past decade have died as martyrs in the company of those they sought to defend, the oppressed people struggled against overwhelming odds. What hope do they have if the bishops, priests, and religious withdraw to the sacristy and restrict themselves to such spiritual functions as baptizing, marrying, and burying?

Yet that is what Puebla prescribes. "The pastors (meaning in the context, bishops), since they should give first consideration to unity, will shed every kind of political and

97

partisan ideology that might condition their judgments and attitudes. . . . The priests, also ministers of unity, and the deacons should accept the very same personal renunciation. . . . The religious . . . should also equally resist the temptation to compromise themselves in party politics, in order not to cause the evangelical values to be confused with a specific ideology." Only in the case of the priests does Puebla envisage possible exceptions, but the kind of exception it envisages is related to situations that arise in the United States or Western Europe, not in Latin America. And it stresses that the "present tendency" of the church is against such exceptions.

All of this official withdrawal of the institutional church in Latin America from the leadership many segments of it have been taking on behalf of the oppressed and powerless since Medellin is music in the ears of the military dictatorships and the international exploiters. As the media they controlled have made clear, they are breathing more freely for having escaped the kind of exposure to world opinion inflicted on them at Medellin. And when oppressive regimes, or the right-wing vigilantes many of them encourage or tolerate, charge priests or religious with inciting the Indians and peasants, and torture, kill, or expel those who resist them, it will be more difficult even for sympathetic bishops to support them. They will be told that Puebla had condemned these priests and religious in advance for disobeying its instructions.

To understand why Puebla adopted this position, one has to analyze the principles it took from the WD, some of them stated explicitly, others emerging from the argument. An important one is its concept of unity as already achieved in Christ and to be guarded in all circumstances. A study both of the gospels and of the world in which we live reveals something quite different. Evangelization as conducted by Jesus implied different conditions for the young rich man and for Philip. Jesus called both to follow him, but he did not hide the difficulties the rich have to overcome in order to follow his call. Jesus did not dialogue with Herod, the oppressor of his powerless fellow-countrymen, nor with Pilate, the representative of the imperial power. Jesus' call to unity does not sidestep the sociopolitical and religious circumstances in which he lived. Jesus creates union in the context of the poor and powerless. When the rich man and the poor man in the parable died, they did not both go to union with God. The rich man went to Hades where he suffered harsh torments. One of the great weaknesses of the Puebla Document is its pretence of a unity that does not exist. Until the reality of our imperfect condition is faced up to, there is no way we can take effective action to correct it.

A similar distorted outlook affects the discussion of violence. Here the ambivalence of the text is notable. Because Medellin had denounced "institutionalized violence" so forthrightly as a situation of injustice widespread in the hemisphere, Puebla could not avoid using the same phrase. But it changes the stress. Having noted a growing deterioration in the political and social state "of our countries," so severe as to produce institutional and economic crises and clear symptoms of corruption and violence, it offers two reasons which it places on an equal level. One is violence institutionalized in various social, political, and economic systems. The other is the ideologies which use violence as a means to seize power. The consequence of this latter kind of violence, it adds, is the spread of regimes based on force (counter-revolutionary), regimes that often draw their inspiration from the Doctrine of National Security. Taking this passage with subsequent statements on the violence of the supporters of the status quo and that of the guerrillas who are fighting unjust regimes, one ends up with the impression that all kinds of violence are the same and that all those engaged in violence are equally to be condemned. The "spiral" of violence comes across as though the original violence is that of the extremists of either the Right or the Left who attack the established government, which replies with counterviolence, only to produce a further intensification of the original violence. The reality of Latin America is that the original violence, as Medellin insisted, is the institutionalized violence with insures that a few get more than their share and the many starve. The next step is the defensive protest of the oppressed which Medellin did not seek to justify but which it insisted was understandable. And the third step is the growth of a system of torture, murder, destruction of homes and crops, either by the regime or vigilantes tolerated by the regime. That Puebla represents a withdrawal is here clear, because the bishops were well aware of the distinction and the reality. It had been affirmed time and again in the years since Medellin. As one important church document put it, "in considering the problem of violence in Latin America, let us by all means avoid equating the *unjust* violence of the oppressors, who maintain this despicable system, with the *just violence* of the oppressed, who feel obliged to use it to achieve their liberation."[6]

The conflicting theological stands just sketched follow logically from different judgments of what is the basic threat to religion in Latin America and what kind of remedy is indicated. The Puebla Document, applying the European experience, sees a loss of faith as the central issue. Now that Latin America is changing from a rural to a predominantly urban society, it is undergoing a process of secularization. The way to counter this, it argues, is to build a new kind of Christendom, a concept to which it returns several times without ever using the word. It recognizes the inevitablity of the worldwide movement from an agricultural and rural to an industrial and urban society, and it proposes that the church can avoid the losses suffered in Europe in this process if it concentrates on infusing a Christian spirit into the new culture that is now developing in Latin America. It envisages a reform of structures along the lines promoted by Christian Democrats as calculated to maintain the allegiance of the masses and gradually to improve economic conditions and provide decent living levels for all.

All of this remains at a highly theoretical level. There is no clear answer to the key question of how this ambitious program is to be implemented in the concrete circumstances of Latin America as a dependent part of the capitalist system. Liberal capitalism and Marxist collectivism are equally condemned as "institutionalized injustice." The modification of capitalism by the adjective "liberal" leaves open the possibility of other acceptable forms of capitalism. We have here no language to match the assertion by Pope Pius X that capitalism is of its nature irreformable because its basic principle is greed.

Puebla did not condemn the theology of liberation, as the more instransigent of the conservatives sought. What it did was to ignore it, and that was logical in the light of its basic presuppositions as just outlined. By centering on the modern spirit of disbelief that characterizes the middle-class societies of Europe, it locates the debate on the philosophical and theological level in the traditional sense of these terms. Liberation Theology, starting from the concrete situation of Latin Americans, sees the central problem as that of the nonperson or nonhuman. This is not meant at the ontological level, but at the existential level, namely, it centers on the many who are considered as nonpersons or nonhumans by a society based on the privilege of a few. Such a formulation of the question focuses attention on the concrete historical condition of the poor and exploited and immediately challenges the class conflict that is inherent in such a society. The majority at Puebla was unwilling to face up to the reality of that class conflict. In consequence, it failed to see that the issue is not directly one of religious belief. The oppressors and the oppressed "share" the same faith. Their conflict is on the economic, social, and political levels.

The Puebla resistance to Liberation Theology comes out very clearly in its treatment of Marxism. The compatibility or

101

incompatibility of Marxism with Christian orthodoxy has been raised by many liberation theologians, as it has also by various European theologians in a different context. The absolute condemnations of Marxism reveal a strange lack of awareness of recent theological reflection and papal statements.

Pope John XXIII in *Pacem in Terris* was the first pope to recognize the fact that "the historical movements that have economic, social, cultural, or political ends" cannot be identified with "the false philosophical teachings regarding the nature, origin, and destiny of people," out of which they have grown.

Pope Paul VI carried this line of thought a significant step farther. In *Octagesima Adveniens*, commemorating the eightieth anniversary of Pope Leo XIII's *Rerum Novarum*, he noted that one of the many forms of Marxism provides a rigorous method of examining social and political reality, thus furnishing some people "not only with a working tool but also a certitude preliminary to action." He properly went on to stress the danger involved in using this tool if the user does not keep clearly in mind "the intimate link" between the Marxist analysis and the other elements of the entire Marxist construct. But he clearly permits its use provided the user takes the indicated precautions.

The Puebla Document misquotes this statement of Paul VI to conclude that a praxis based on the Marxist analysis brings "the total politicization of Christian experience, the dissolution of the language of faith into the language of the social sciences, and the emptying of the transcendental dimension of Christian salvation." That is not its only misquotation in its concern to reject the class struggle. It appeals to *Acts* 10:38 in support of its claim that Jesus loved all *without distinction*, a contention that the text does not support.

It is easy to condemn liberal capitalism and Marxist collectivism, as these systems concretely exist in the world today, as constituting "institutionalized injustice" and "systems of sin." But of what use is that to the oppressed and powerless millions of Americans if they are offered no viable alternative? The closest thing to an answer in the Puebla Document is the suggestion that ultimately love will triumph and the oppressors will be converted and share with those they have oppressed. There are many fine words, much righteous indignation, but they all add up to pie in the sky.

The liberation theologians have a more realistic understanding of human nature and a more convincing interpretation of the way Jesus faced, and called on his followers to face, the reality of evil in the world. Puebla speaks piously about "unity and communion in the church," about Jesus as the universal reconciler. What is missing is a realistic appreciation of the significance of the generalized, lasting, and institutionalized injustice and violence—nowhere more visible than in Latin America. This means that reconciliation cannot occur without our passing through the same conflict as Jesus, which is what the liberation theologians are trying to tell us.

11. No Turning Back

Puebla has focused world attention on the church in Latin America and its growing importance both to the universal church and to the outcome of the life-and-death struggle of the hemisphere's masses to create a human society. The pope's visit contributed to this awareness. But it had already been assured by the response to the Preliminary Document issued more than a year earlier by the CELAM secretariat. And it was reinforced by the army of journalists and the concerned groups who thronged to Puebla during the meeting and demonstrated by word and action what they hoped to see the conference achieve.

The conference itself and the entire process it triggered defined more clearly than before that—in spite of the verbal insistence on unity—the church in Latin America is deeply divided by two irreconcilable understandings of what is the nature and function of the church. This division affects not only the hierarchy but cuts through the entire body of adherents. In simplest terms, one ecclesiology stresses the vertical relationship of people to God, with the church as mediator and channel of grace to proclaim truth and impose detailed moral rules, the place of each in the hierarchy clearly defined. The other stresses the horizontal relationship, with Saint John the Apostle seeing God concretely in the neighbor and placing the essence of religion in love expressed in action on behalf of the oppressed neighbor.[1]

Latin America demonstrates the significance of the distinction. Those of its inhabitants who live in such abject misery that they are nonhumans, if not already a majority, will be such within a decade if present trends persist. The term is to be understood existentially, not ontologically. They are members of the human race, but society does not recognize them as such, feels no obligation to insure their right to food, clothing, shelter, health, education, and dignity. Other than the Philippines, Latin America is the only part of the world of poverty, of the nonhuman world, that identifies society as formed under predominantly Roman Catholic influences. The Puebla Document stresses these Christian roots. The church must consequently accept a large share of the responsibility for the nonhuman situation and concentrate on living the fullness of the gospel of truth with those whom Jesus loved preferentially and whose lot he shared while trying to improve it.

Recognizing this priority, Liberation Theology insists that it is irrelevant to discuss the questions about God of the nonbeliever on which traditional theology concentrates. Rather, as Gustavo Gutiérrez defines it: "These nonhumans do not call into question our religious world so much as they call into question our economic, social, political and cultural world. Their challenge impels us toward a revolutionary transformation of the very bases of what is now a dehumanizing society. The question, then, is no longer how we are to speak about God in a world come of age; it is rather how to proclaim him Father in a world that is not human, and what the implications might be of telling nonhumans they are children of God."[2]

Some of the methods used by some conservatives, as described in earlier chapters, shed little credit on their understanding of their role as religious leaders. The unfortunate reality is that one finds in church assemblies, as in all situations in which humans are involved (even when the Spirit is present to guide), a mixture of motives and an element of pragmatism.

This should not be exaggerated, however, to the point of excluding the positive reasons for conflicting stands. There is no cause to doubt that subjectively convincing reasons determined the decisions and votes of the conference members. It may help if we look at a few of the considerations that influenced those who resist change, believe the old ways were right, and insist that they will still work with only superficial modernization.

In Chapter 3 we described the training of all today's Latin American bishops in Roman theology, and in Chapter 4 the perennial alliance of influential church leaders and members with the structures of society now admitted universally to be unjust and unChristian. It is not possible, sociologically speaking, for most people so thoroughly conditioned, to break out of that conditioning, especially when a break would be not only shattering to one's self-image but also a threat to vested interests. All these factors are here present. It is not easy for bishops who are convinced that God has imposed on them the duty to preserve intact the revealed truths and to tell the people what is right and wrong to accept the possibility of a church in which decisions are made collegially by consensus, and in which each member is encouraged to read the signs of the times and to judge and act accordingly. In addition, many of them cannot conceive how they could possibly maintain the institution they feel it is their duty to maintain without continuing the traditional alliances with the powerful to protect the wealth and influence they judge basic to the functioning of the church.

This mental framework also helps us to understand why the Puebla Document reasserted a clerical-lay dichotomy—objectively not compatible with Vatican Council II—and withdrew the clergy from the "political" area (in the sense described in Chapter 10). Yet these actions are not only theologically questionable. They do not represent political realism. In most of Latin America today, the church is the sole surviving institution capable of challenging injustices with some degree of effectiveness. The oppressed people retain their trust and hope in it. But to the extent that the church withdraws from the role of protector and leader, it is inevitable that such trust and hope will decline. The ecstatic response to the pope's presence was evidence that the people want and expect the church's leadership. But, as we learned from many of the committed Christians who voiced their hopes and concerns in Puebla, many are no longer prepared to be patient as their parents and grandparents were.

Some bishops may have thought that by discouraging the political activities in which many priests have involved themselves since Vatican II, they would have more personnel available to maintain the traditional system of sacramental service, relying on the "religiosity" of the people to keep them faithful to the church. This argument is persuasive. Given the vast and growing numbers of the baptized and the relative scarcity of priests, the task of providing the intellectual and moral formation to permit each individual to make a personal commitment would be excessive. The argument, nevertheless, is fallacious. Even if all priests available were committed to the traditional sacramental services, they would not for long be sufficient to maintain them. The history of the priesthood in Latin America since Medellin explains why. It is true that a not inconsiderable number of priests have been deported because of their identification with the people. But their number is insignificant in comparison with the number who have abandoned the ministry, a total of 20,000 in a decade, that is to say, two of every five. Such a phenomenon has many causes, but a principal one was a sense that the church structures prevented the priest from exercising the social ministry demanded by the needs of the people. With few exceptions, seminaries have experienced and continue to experience a relative, and often an absolute, decline in ordinations. With a similar decline in most of the countries that have been providing half of all priests working in Latin America, there is no way to take up the slack. Some easing of the situation might be affected by ordaining married men and by ordaining women. Puebla made clear it would not even consider those approaches.

Regardless of the desires of the bishops, however, the weight of events is going to declericalize the church in Latin America ever further. Everything points to the continued growth of the *comunidades de base*. The fact that the "new ministers" they are developing will not be ordained will shift the emphasis from church as a series of sacrament service stations to ministry of people one to another. The result will be a church significantly different from the Roman model that has dominated the Latin church since the sixteenth century. As such, it will be a pilot project in adapting the church to cultures other than European, something that Vatican II judged inevitable and desirable.

Puebla struggled hard with the concept of popular religion or "religiosity," but with so many different understandings and ambiguities as never to reach concrete conclusions. Religiosity covers a host of overlapping situations, syncretisms of Christianity with African and American Indian religions, distortions of Catholic teaching that glorify the Virgin and different saints to the effective ignoring of Jesus the Savior and Liberator, attributing of magical powers to shrines and other objects of devotion. While admitting the seriousness of the distortions, many church leaders—both conservative and progressive—have come in recent years to give more stress than previously to the positive elements in popular religion. The Puebla Document continues this trend.

In doing so, however, it overlooks an essential aspect, namely, the reasons why popular religion is so important to the people. They are poor and they are oppressed. Their faith helps them to endure and to struggle. The Document ignores their oppression and speaks only of the poor as believers, pointing to secularism as the danger to their faith. This is to look at Latin America from a European perspective. It assumes that as the rural people are swept by economic need into the amorphous slums mushrooming around the cities, they will become secularized in the same way as happened in Europe earlier.

What is happening is quite different. The rapidity and totality of the uprooting that moves people through thousands of years of culture in a single bus or truck ride produces such feelings of anomie and insecurity as to make them cling desperately to remnants of the old society, especially religious rites.

It has therefore to be realized that the priests and others who are dispensing Christian rites in packed churches are, as Juan Luis Segundo has pointed out, "dispensing security, just as the shaman or witch doctor of a primitive tribe does." But religiosity based on insecurity no longer assures transmission of Christianity from generation to generation. Today, the mass media have replaced parents and schools as inculcators of values for children and adolescents. Their influence does not necessarily exclude a vague and nebulous adherence to Christianity; but they cannot be regarded sociologically as a guarantee that a Christian conception of life will be transmitted from generation to generation. "The milieu no longer generates or substitutes for real personal conviction," Segundo concludes. "A church wholly submerged in providing people with security does not have the time or personnel to fashion new methods and approaches that would replace the closed milieus of the past with a Christianity based on real personal conviction."[3]

There is an underlying reason for the Document's repeated diversion of attention from oppression to secularism. It wants to ignore the class conflict that is a central issue for church and society. On this point the Document is schizophrenic. In its messages to the peoples of Latin America, it denounces the paradox of a system that constantly increases the distance between the many who have little and the few who have much. This poverty, they continue, "is not a transitional stage but rather the product of economic, social, and political structures and situations that are its cause." This statement followed logically from what John Paul had said to the Indians at Oaxaca, namely, that their situation resulted from "structures of sin in which our personal, family and social life are trapped."

Yet whenever the Document comes to solutions, all this is forgotten. When evangelization priorities are discussed—and evangelization is the central theme and purpose of the meeting—the primary concern is to evangelize the culture, identifying the problem as the secularization of the culture, not the oppression of the poor. That is to substitute a cultural for a sociopolitical analysis. As long as the present process of isolating the people from their political and social roots continues, any discussion of culture is abstract. And since it would be anachronistic to attempt to return to a rural society that is not today viable, the only way to encourage and gradually purify popular religion is through the *comunidades de base*. Again, Puebla gave its blessing to these, but in a form that suggests a desire to modify their structures and establish a control from the top down. For reasons set out in Chapter 2, the movement will be successful only to the extent that initiative comes from below and within. It is for the bishops a serious dilemma.

The neurotic resistance to any recognition of the conflict that is the most obvious phenomenon of contemporary Latin America was already clear in the Document voted by the bishops. The rewriting in Rome stressed this aberration further. Perhaps its purpose is to discourage the growing number of committed Christians, including not a few priests and nuns, who apply in practice the principles of Catholic theology regarding the right to self-defense against unjust attack and the Christian duty to protect the helpless. But one can suspect that another reason coexists, namely, a concern to avoid any expression that could be interpreted as favoring liberation theology.

But how can this silence be reconciled with the prophetic mission of the church? It is easy to condemn liberal capitalism and Marxist collectivism, as these systems exist concretely in today's world, as "institutionalized injustice" and "systems of sin." But of what use is that to the poor and oppressed millions of Latin Americans if they are offered no viable alternative? The Document refers repeatedly to what it calls the social doctrine of the church as offering a "third way" that is neither capitalist nor Marxist. All that comes through in the Document, however, is an exhortation to the oppressed to accept their lot with "Christian" resignation until the wealthy and powerful finally see the light and are good to them.

That, of course, even if were to happen—and all history denies its possibility—would not liberate the poor. Liberation by someone else is only a change of masters. We would still have a class that rules and a class that is ruled. At its kindest interpretation, the Document is proposing a reform of the capitalistic system that Pope Saint Pius X—no radical he—proclaimed to be irremediably evil because based essentially on greed and brute power. To favor reform of that system is to be subtly for it, as Gustavo Gutiérrez has pointed out, since "only a clear break with the unjust order and a frank commitment to a new society can make the Christian message of love credible to Latin Americans."[4]

Puebla was not an end in itself, but rather a moment of reflection and discussion on where the church is and where it should concentrate its limited resources. For a proper understanding of Puebla, according to Brazilian theologian Leonardo Boff, we should note several aspects. It was a conference, not a council. The binding force on bishops of its decisions is moral, not legal. It was a meeting of bishops, not an assembly of the entire People of God of Latin America. Only some of

Latin America's bishops attended as representatives of the others, so that it was not a plenary conference. The processes for choosing *periti* (experts) and other non-elected members were—in Boff's words—"judged by many as 'questionable.' " The more than 300 participants did not have time to treat tranquilly and adequately 21 themes presented in more than 200 pages. The final document represents the average level of awareness of the episcopate, not the level of the most sensitized members. The meeting was not an isolated event but the culmination of a 2-year reflection in which the entire church took part and expressed itself in countless commentaries and actions.

The meeting in the Palofoxian Seminary was, as Boff correctly observes, an episcopal conference. But it must be related to the meetings already described held simultaneously in Puebla, in which priests, nuns, lay people, and some of the conference bishops and various other bishops participated. These meetings, the Puebla "event," were ecclesial. Taken in conjunction with the advance reflection and action, they evidence the presence of the Spirit in the Latin American church.

To complete the context, other elements must be noted. Medellin occurred at a time when the hemispheric political scene was relatively tranquil and church-state relations were good. The bishops were anxious to implement Vatican Council II, and those who dominated the meeting were clearly identified with the hopes of the poor, working harmoniously with *periti* who today are identified as the first to formulate the theology of liberation. Puebla brought together representatives of a church that has experienced ten years of martyrdom as a result of the application by many of its members of the principles enunciated by Medellin. The violent response of governments and other power holders had in turn provoked revolutionary movements which claimed that the oppressed were entitled to use counterviolence.

The CELAM secretariat, charged with preparing the position papers for Puebla, was dominated by people who believed it would be a disaster for the church to repeat and strengthen Medellin's call for liberation of the oppressed. The result, they believed, would be more persecution for the church and more suffering for the poor. They believed that prudence called for a deemphasis on the *comunidades de base*, and a condemnation of the Liberation Theology as a kind of Trojan Horse bringing Marxist errors into the church. Instead, they proposed a division of activities. The state would concern itself with the material welfare of the poor, and the church would concentrate on promoting Christian cultural values. Bishops and theologians who opposed this program were to be marginalized as attempting to set up a "parallel magisterium."

These concerns and this policy dominated the PD and the WD, and many of the elements survive in the final Puebla Document. The secretariat opened the meeting full of confidence. Its influence on the selection of the conference members, including the voting members, had insured that the progressives were a minority, no more than a third of the voters, and the secretariat's supporters constituted a solid and structurally cohesive bloc. Pope John Paul's speeches in Mexico, with their stress on traditional theology and their warnings against novelties and deviations gave them further cause to be confident. What they underestimated was the progressive social message that accompanied the traditional theology, especially in the pope's talks in Oaxaca and Guadalajara. With the help of the theologians who had been excluded from the meeting but who had nevertheless come to Puebla, the progressives were able to use the papal statements and the Medellin documents so effectively as to stalemate the counterattack. In the final analysis, Medellin has been retained in its broad thrust. The importance of the *comunidades de base* has been reaffirmed. The theology of liberation survives as an orthodox option. As explained in the previous chapter, some of the Puebla statements were further watered down by revisions made before the promulgation by Rome of the official text. Enough remains, nevertheless, to justify those who seek to continue the social direction sanctioned at Medellin as expressing the directives and spirit of Vatican Council II. And just as the Medellin meeting was only an element in a process, so that the dynamic upsurge that followed the meeting was what really determined the new directions, in the same way the real significance of Puebla will be determined by the practical pastoral applications that follow. What is important is that no door has been closed.

For the next decade we can expect a continuation of the two mutually exclusive ways of being church that characterized—as described earlier—the decade since Medellin. The intensification of economic and political struggles in most countries of the hemisphere can only accelerate the movement of growing numbers of Christians to opt openly for the oppressed and take the consequences. In spite of Puebla's reservations, this group will include many priests and nuns and some bishops. Meanwhile, the continuing decline in the personnel willing to continue the traditional function of administering the sacraments will leave the institution with the options of declining further or of undertaking bold new initiatives for which it showed no enthusiasm in Puebla.

The ability of the institution to update will be seriously influenced by the turnover of bishops year by year. If forward-looking men are named and placed in key positions, obviously the transition will be easier. Several recent events, however, are not reassuring. The choice of López Trujillo as president of CELAM two months after the Puebla meeting and of the conservative Brazilian archbishop (recipient of the letter revealing his plans to manipulate the conference) as secretary general determines the role of that important institution for the next several years. Some observers had anticipated that the creation of four regional organizations (see Chapter 3) would lead to lessening of the importance of CELAM and the devolution to the regions of many of its functions. López Trujillo has already shown he has no such intention. A meeting of the Brazilian bishops held shortly after his election received a letter from CELAM directing the Brazilian bishops not to sponsor any evaluation of the Puebla Document without first notifying CELAM and receiving from it guidelines for correct interpretation and implementation. It is doubtful that the Brazilian bishops will accept such instructions. One bishop commented that it looked as if a second Curia was in process of creation on this side of the Atlantic.[5] But smaller episcopal conferences, more dependent on Roman aid, will have difficulty in rejecting the proposals of one who is clearly in the good graces of the Roman Curia.

And even Brazil has cause for concern because of the way in which recent appointments and transfers of bishops have occurred. Some four years ago, the Conference of Brazilian Bishops set up permanent regional commissions of bishops to recommend candidates, a procedure that has been introduced worldwide since Vatican II. Their notification to the nuncio did not even receive the courtesy of a reply. Candidates recommended by these commissions have been consistently passed over. Ignoring Cardinal Lorscheider, head of the conference, and Cardinal Arns of São Paulo, the nuncio gets advice exclusively from two or three conservative archbishops. A European-born priest was named bishop in 1979 to a diocese whose clergy, with the support of the regional commission of bishops, had unanimously recommended a universally esteemed Brazilian priest. This year also, the priests of another diocese were so outraged by the bishop imposed on them that 85 percent of them voted to withdraw from the diocese. Another priest recently named bishop had earlier to leave his own diocese when it was learned that he had delated his bishop to the secret police for his "political views." He is a member of Faith, Fatherland, and Tradition, an ultrarightist vigilante movement against which both the Vatican and the Brazilian bishops have issued warning in recent years.

An article in the May 1979 issue of the prestigious French Catholic news magazine *Informations Catholiques Internationales* blames Cardinal Baggio, head of the Congregation for Bishops and a former nuncio to Brazil, as responsible for this "vendetta" against the Brazilian hierarchy because of the courageous stands it has taken in recent years.

These are not encouraging signs. They do nothing for the church's credibility. Yet it may be just such obvious abuses of power that are needed to arouse opinion in the church both in Latin America and around the world to the reality of the agony of a hemisphere nailed by other nations that call themselves Christian to the cross of hunger and oppression.

The Latin Americans have not given up hope that through the cross will come resurrection. Theologian Sergio Torres spoke for many when he concluded his depressing account of what happened at Puebla with these brave words: "I was part of a group of Latin American theologians working outside the Conference as advisors to some bishops participating in the Conference. I witnessed a beautiful experience. The Spirit of God was present there. The suffering, struggles, and hope of the poor were stronger than the manipulations against Medellin. History will go on. Puebla will be remembered as a moment of the saving presence of Jesus. We have to be grateful for this wonderful gift."

The Puebla meeting was not long over when evidences began to appear that Sergio Torres was not mistaken in his belief that the Spirit was at work. In April 1979, the bishop of David, Panama, issued a very strong protest against the multinational corporations that were ignoring the rights of the Indians in their proposed development of what is claimed to be the world's biggest copper deposit. A month later all nine Panamanian bishops joined his protest, noting specifically that Puebla's preferential option for the poor, as well as its warnings against the abuses of the multinationals justified their intervention.

About the same time, the bishops of Nicaragua issued a joint pastoral affirming specifically the moral and legal right of the people to overthrow by force "a visible and long-endured tyranny." That action undoubtedly hastened the final elimination of Somoza. Elsewhere in Central America, Archbishop Romero of San Salvador and other church leaders expressed support for the struggle in Nicaragua and condemned the continuing oppression in their countries. All of this can only be interpreted as an indication that what will survive and bear fruit from Puebla is what moves the church and society along the road to liberation.

The United States also has felt the influence. At the May 1979 meeting of the National Conference of Catholic Bishops, Archbishop John Quinn (its president) made a specific reference to Latin America. In a prophetic statement that echoed the very words he had heard spoken by Pope John Paul II in Mexico, words reaffirmed in the Puebla Document, he said: "The oppression of the many by a minority of powerful and entrenched local governments and private interests, and particularly when the oppressor and the oppressed are both Catholic, can only be described as a sin against the Creator and desecration of the human person."

Stands on human rights by members of the United States hierarchy have not always been prophetic. People who know Archbishop Quinn have observed a marked change of attitude and emphasis since his experience with John Paul and the Puebla meeting. His leadership of his fellow bishops along this road could start fifty million United States Catholics to reflect on our society's need for atonement and reconciliation. The kind of political pressures this would generate could trigger more ethical and moral national policies in Latin America and also at home. To reflect on the reality of the hemisphere in the light of the church's potential as demonstrated by the pope's visit helps us to see more clearly glaring issues of injustice that for lack of attention grow like weeds in our nation. Hopefully, we United States Christians will be challenged to go beyond such bandaiding as providing homes for Vietnam's boat people, refugees from Chile, Argentina, Nicaragua, and the millions of undocumented within our borders, to look more questioningly at the system that generates such exploitation and misery.

The dynamic of Puebla was even more evident at the Eighth Annual Conference of the Notre Dame Center for Pastoral Liturgy, June 1978. Developing the theme, "Service: Community Prayer and Community Justice," the coordinators proclaimed that the time is right in the church "to confront ourselves seriously with the relationship between the liturgy and the world." Jesuit Walter J. Burghardt, a theologian at Catholic University and editor of *Theological Studies*, described the controversial liturgy on Argentina's national day at St. Matthew's Cathedral in Washington (May 1979) as an heroic example of Karl Rahner's thesis that the church must exhibit "the courage for concrete imperatives and concrete directives, even in regard to social and political action by Christians in the world."

Burghardt recalled how the homilist, a former missionary in Argentina, quoted John Paul II and the Latin American bishops on repression, torture, disappearances, and their rejection of the efforts by governments to justify such activities on the basis of national security. He then focused on the people who had vanished under the Videla regime and likened the situation to Herod's slaughter of the innocents. The embassy officials, military leaders, and other Argentine adherents of the regime stormed angrily out of the church, damning the homilist for turning a religious into a political event. Not so, concluded Burghardt. Even if the church's essential role is religious, that "does not exempt the people of God from the ceaseless struggle to transform the city of man into the kingdom of God."

Auxiliary Bishop Thomas Gumbleton of Detroit, president of Bread for the World and of Pax Christi, spoke of the "immense network of institutional sin" that fails to disturb most Catholics. If we really understood the evangelizing task that is ours as self-proclaimed Christians, the kind of question we would be asking ourselves is: "Do not these oppressed Latin Americans—Catholics—have something against us?"[6]

Protestants as well as Catholics in the United States seem to be hearing this message from Puebla. Synodal meetings of Lutherans, Presbyterians, Methodists, Episcopalians, and others, seem in 1979 to have called more insistently for justice and stood more firmly against oppression. An area of particular concern has been the situation of undocumented people in the United States, with serious efforts to develop an immigrant policy that would treat every individual as a human being and not simply as an economic unit.

Seen in this light, Puebla is a parable with enormous meaning for us. Unlike a story with a happy but usually superficial ending, a parable contains an unresolved dialectic. It does not conform to our sense of propriety. The tares grow along with the wheat. The meek inherit the earth. One obvious challenge of the Puebla parable is that the forgotten Christians of poverty-stricken lands are here bringing liberation to those who thought little of them or at best felt good by throwing to them a few crumbs from their rich table. Yet it is precisely they who now have a message, the good news of liberation, for us. Replacing the great, the powerful, and the learned, the poor, the weak, and the unlettered—always the preferred of Jesus—are finally assuming their historic role as the church born of the people.

Notes

For Books and documents not fully identified in these Notes, check Bibliography.

Chapter 1

1. Third World activities of global corporations are concentrated to the extent of 76 percent in Latin America, according to Xabier Gorostiaga, in *Para Entender América Latina*, p. 210. For a fuller account of the destructive impact of the globals, see Barnet and Muller, *Global Reach* and Ledogar, *Hungry for Profits*.

2. *São Paulo: Growth and Poverty*.

3. See Dussel, *History and the Theology of Liberation*, pp. 75–109.

Chapter 2

1. José Comblin is the theologian who has studied most deeply the Doctrine of National Security. His central conclusions are in "The Church and the National Security System," in LADOC, VI, 28, May-June 1976; also in "La Doctrina de la seguridad nacional," *Mensaje* (Santiago, Chile), 1976, 247, pp. 96–104 (English version in LADOC IX, 4, March–April 1979). For a quick overview, Gary Mac-Eoin's "A Continent in Agony," *The Progressive*, March 1979.

2. Eduardo Hoornaert and Leonardo Boff give two excellent accounts of the grassroots community movement in Brazil, in *Revista Eclesiastica Brasileira*, # 151, Sept. 1978.

3. Freire's *The Pedagogy of the Oppressed* (New York: Herder and Herder, 1970) remains the best introduction to his thought.

4. *The Church in the Present Day Transformation of Latin America in the Light of the Council* (Washington, D.C.: U.S. Catholic

Conference) is the official English translation of the Medellin Documents. Virgilio P. Elizondo gives a quick summary of their content in *Christianity and Culture* (Huntingdon, Ind.: Our Sunday Visitor, 1975), pp. 102–112.

5. In *Concilium* 96, 1974, published in U.S. by Seabury Press. *A Theology of Liberation*, by Gutiérrez is still the best systematic overview of the movement.

6. See Note 2, above.

7. These accounts of the Ajusco Encounter and of the description by Sister Elena Martínez of conditions in Cuernavaca's industrial park are from our own tape recordings and those of a Canadian Broadcasting Company television unit for which we acted as consultants and interpreters.

Chapter 3

1. For a documented account of this seminary formation, see Gary MacEoin, *The Inner Elite: Dossiers of Papal Candidates* (Kansas City: Sheed, Andrews and McMeel, 1978).

2. A major source for all these developments is LADOC (Latin American Documentation); a series published six times a year by the U.S. Catholic Conference, Washington, D.C. A key document is *I Have Heard the Cries of My People*, a statement by the bishops of Brazil's Northeast (New York: IDOC-America, 54, 1973). Other major sources are the collection of church statements in *Between Honesty and Hope* (Maryknoll N.Y.: Orbis Books, 1970), Dussel's *History and the Theology of Liberation*, MacEoin's *Revolution Next Door*, and *Latin America in Search of Liberation*, an issue of *Cross Currents* (XXI, 3, Summer 1971) edited by MacEoin.

Chapter 4

1. Dussel, *History and the Theology of Liberation*, pp. 82–85.

2. See "Liberation Praxis and Christian Faith," by Gustavo Gutiérrez, in *Frontiers of Theology*, Gibellini, ed., pp. 1–32.

3. Commentators on the Final Document of Puebla have noted that it stresses Mary's awareness in the Magnificat, that Jesus, her son, would radically alter the social system, not only raising up the powerless but ejecting from their high places the oppressors.

4. "There is a growing awareness of the sublime dignity of the

human person, who stands above all things, and whose rights and duties are universal and inviolable. Each ought, therefore, to have a ready access to what is necessary for living a genuinely human life; for example, food, clothing, housing, the right to choose a state of life and set up a family, the right to education, work, good name, respect, proper knowledge, the right to act according to the dictates of conscience and to safeguard privacy, and rightful freedom also in religious matters. The social order and its development must constantly yield to the good of the person, since the order of things must be subordinated to the order of persons and not the other way round, as the Lord suggested when he said the Sabbath was made for man and not man for the Sabbath. The social order requires constant improvement; it must be founded in truth, built on justice, and enlivened by love; it should grow in freedom toward a more human equilibrium." Vatican II, "The Church in the Modern World," 1965, #26.

5. See Pablo Richard, "The Latin American Church, 1959–1978" in *Cross Currents*, XXVII, 1, pp. 34–36, esp. p. 45.

6. Text of *Pacem in Terris* in Gremillion, *The Gospel of Peace and Justice*. For a fuller discussion of this important issue, see MacEoin's "Forming a Catholic Conscience on Social Questions," *Cross Currents*, XXV, 2, Summer 1975. This Study had earlier been delivered at the American Catholic Bishops' Bicentennial hearing in Washington, D.C.

7. This evaluation is based on personal observation and discussion by both authors in Cuba. See also MacEoin's "Cuba at Work," *The Progressive*, March 1978.

Chapter 5

1. Many of these are reproduced or described in the special issues of *Cross Currents, IDOC-International*, and other magazines and news services, the addresses of which are given in the Bibliography.

2. *Cross Currents*, XXVIII, 1, p. 71.

3. The seriousness of this confusion regarding the multiplicity of cultures in Latin America is brought out by a group of Peruvian theologians in a statement in *Cross Currents*, XXVIII, 1, p. 49.

4. See *Repression Against the Church in Brazil, 1968–1978* (Centro Ecumenico de Documentacão e Informacão, rua Cosme

Velho 98, fundos, Cosme Velho, Rio de Janeiro, RJ, Brazil), Dec. 1978. Also *São Paulo: Growth and Poverty*, and "A Continent in Agony," *The Progressive*, March 1979.

5. "Many parts of Latin America are experiencing a situation of injustice that can be called institutionalized injustice. The structures of industry and agriculture, of the national and international economy, the cultural and political life all violate fundamental rights. Entire peoples lack the bare necessities and live in a condition of such dependency that they can exercise neither initiative nor responsibility. Similarly, they lack all possibility of cultural improvement and of participation in social and political life. Such situations call for global, daring, urgent, and basically renewing change. It should surprise nobody that the temptation to violence should manifest itself in Latin America. It is wrong to abuse the patience of people who have endured for years a situation that would have been intolerable if they were more aware of their rights as human beings." *Documentos finales de Medellin* (Buenos Aires: Ediciones Paulinas, 1969), p. 191 ff.

6. Lorscheider: Introductory note to PD.

7. As recently as the first Conference of Latin American Bishops in 1955, at which CELAM was created, the major concerns of the meeting were two: a shortage of priests, and the aggressive inroads of Protestantism.

8. In *Theology of Liberation* (p. 72) Gutiérrez traces the term "New Christendom" to Jacques Maritain in *True Humanism* (New York: Charles Scribner Sons, 1938). He rejects equally the earlier model of "Christendom" in which "the church is regarded substantially as the exclusive depository of salvation" (p. 53) and the Maritain model stressing the autonomy of the temporal sphere with regard to the church, arguing that it often masked a tacit alliance of the church with oppressive regimes and was utterly inadequate to deal with the enormous misery and injustice universal in Latin America. Instead, he opts for "a single vocation to salvation.... that gives religious value in a completely new way to the action of humans in history, Christians and non-Christians alike" (p. 72).

9. A typical quote from *The Church in the Modern World*: "The church, at once a visible organization and a spiritual community, travels the same journey as all mankind and shares the same earthly lot with the world: it is to be a leaven and as it were, the soul

of human society in its renewal by Christ and transformation into the family of God. . . . The Church, then, believes it can contribute much to humanizing the family of man and its history through each of its members and its community as a whole. . . . Similarly, it is convinced that there is a considerable and varied help that it can receive in preparing the ground for the Gospel, both from individuals and from society as a whole, by their talents and activity." (Par. 40).

Chapter 6

1. See Note 1 to Chapter 5.
2. This document, dated Sept. 1978, was distributed in Spanish translation by CRIE Documentation (Aptdo. Postal 85–13, Mexico 20 D.F.).
3. *Excelsior*, Mexico, D.F. 10 August 1977.
4. English versions published by LADOC.
5. Addresses in Bibliography, also addresses of *Cross Currents* and IDOC, referred to below.
6. *Latinamerica Press*, 15 June 1978.
7. *Latinamerica Press*, 12 Oct., 1978.

Chapter 7

1. Actually, the nonvoting members were allowed to speak in the committees but not in the general sessions. Lack of time was given by López Trujillo as the reason for this administrative decision.

Chapter 8

1. Good summary in *Los Angeles Times* supplement on Mexico, 15 July 1979 in article entitled, "The Church Today: a Rich Ritual, a Nominal Faith," by Patt Morrison.
2. J.B. Libanio in "Celam III: Fears and Hopes" (*Cross Currents*, XXVIII, 1).
3. For more about the transnational or global corporations, see books listed in note 1 to Chapter 1. See also *Food First*, by Moore Lappé and Collins.
4. For descriptions of some major slums, see MacEoin's *Revolution Next Door*, pp. 4, 98, 208. For subsequent deterioration see his "A Contingent in Agony," *The Progressive*, March 1979, and *São Paulo: Growth and Poverty*.

5. Gary MacEoin, *The Inner Elite* (Kansas City: Sheed Andrews and McMeel, 1978), p. 172.

6. In his general audience in Rome, 21 February 1979, John Paul spoke approvingly of the theology of liberation. He referred not only to the Latin American exponents but also to the European Hans von Balthasar, "who rightly calls for a theology of liberation of universal application." It should be noted, however, that the approach of von Balthasar—in the European tradition of reasoning from principles to conclusions—is significantly different from that of the Latin Americans who begin with a sociological evaluation of their lived reality and then turn to Scripture to discover what answers it offers for the problems they have identified. Full text of this address in *Servir*, XV, 79. Complete text of all John Paul's statements in Mexico published as *Discursos de Juan Pablo II en Mexico* by CENCOS. *Time* (8 Feb. 1979) has excellent summary of events and significance of pope's visit. See also *Latinamerica Press* 1 Feb. 1979. Pope's public statement in Rome can be found in *Com Nuovi Tempi*, Rome, 25 Feb. 1979; and in *Vida Nueva*, 3 Mar 1979. No. 1169, p. 32.

7. Summa Theologica, 2, 2ae, Q. 66, A. 2. For the development of the church's teaching on the social function and use of private property from the Middle Ages to the present time, see Gremillion, *Gospel of Peace*, pp. 27–35. For a distortion introduced by Leo XIII in *Rerum Novarum* and corrected by Vatican Council II, see Gary MacEoin *What Happened at Rome?* (New York: Holt, Rinehart and Winston, 1966), p. 111.

8. *Christology at the Crossroads.*

9. *Puebla 1979*, Theology in the Americas Documentation Series, # 7, p. 14 (475 Riverside Drive, New York 10027).

Chapter 9

1. See "Writers Telling the Puebla Story in Spite of Obstacles" and "Velvet Curtain Shields Bishops at Puebla," *Latinamerica Press* 8 and 15 Feb. 1979.

2. Many of the texts presented by the various groups, as well as the texts of the beautiful songs that constitute the Nicaraguan "Peasant Mass" have been published by CENCOS.

3. All these position papers obtainable from Mujeres Para el Diálogo, Aptdo. Postal 579, Cuernavaca (Mor.), Mexico. A continu-

ing "working group" was formed at Puebla; its members, Victoria Reyes, Peru; Leonor Aida Concha, Cuernavaca, and Ann Gabriel Marciacq, Tucson, Arizona.

Chapter 10

1. "Christ summons the church, as she goes her pilgrim way, to that continual reformation of which she has always need." Vatican Council II, *Decree on Ecumenism*, par. 6.

2. *NTC News* (00184 Roma, via Firenze 38, Italy), VI, 5, 15 March 1979. Analysis of changes in *Informations Catholiques Internationales* (163 bd Malesherbes, 75849 Paris, Cedex 17), No. 540, p. 18.

3. "It is important, first of all, to note the very diverse meanings applied to the term 'ideology.' The more usual connotation is a pejorative one, referring to a mental mechanism that serves certain class, race, or other interests by concealing or sacralizing a given situation. . . . However, the term can also be understood in a more *neutral* sense, that is, as a person's basic system of goals and values, plus the means to achieve them. And this neutral sense applies to both religious and secular areas." Hennelly, *Theologies in Conflict*, p. 173.

4. *Medellin Documents*, # 8–18.

5. *Medellin Documents*, # 4–5.

6. "Continent of Violence" in *Between Honesty and Hope*, p. 84.

Chapter 11

1. Hennelly explores this issue thoroughly in *Theologies in Conflict*. "The preservation of unity is often viewed as a supreme value which must take precedence over any historical divisions that may actually exist among the members on basic issues. By thus making unity an absolute, however, the church is forced into the position of holding 'that the issues of suffering, violence, hunger, and death are less critical than religious formulas or rites.' Moreover, the unity achieved takes place only at the level of language; for if 'one person conceives of a God who permits dehumanization, while another rejects such a God and believes only in a God who struggles unceasingly against such things,' then the obvious conclusion is that they do not really believe in the same God or share the same faith." P. 11. See also pp. 87–92. The phrases quoted in above extract from Hen-

nelly are from Juan Luis Segundo's *The Liberation of Theology* (Maryknoll, N.Y.: Orbis Books, 1976).

2. *Concilium*, 96, 1974. English edition published by Seabury Press, New York.

3. *Cross Currents* XXVIII, 1, p. 106.

4. Report of Gutiérrez press conference in Puebla during Bishops' Meeting. CRIE: 4–79–5–000–459.

5. *Informations Catholiques Internationales*, No. 538.

6. Excellent summary of conference in *AD Correspondence* (Notre Dame, Ind. 46556), XIX, 1, 14 July 1979.

Bibliography

Commentaries

(Commentaries on the preparations for Puebla and evaluations of the meeting and its results are scattered in hundreds of magazines and special bulletins in many languages. Listed here are some of the more important and more readily obtainable.

Fichas Informativas (Pax Romana, Apdo. Postal 20–145, Mexico 20 D.F.)

Communicaciones Cencos (Medellin 33, Col. Roma, Mexico 7, D.F.)

Informaciones Ecumenicas (CRIE, Ocotepec 39, San Jeronimo, Mexico 20 D.F.)

CRIE has also published every report of everything related to Pope John Paul's visit (including his speeches) and to the Puebla meeting that appeared in any Mexico City or Puebla newspaper. It has also published a bibliography of nearly a thousand books, documents, articles and news reports published around the world from August 1977 to January 1979 on the preparations for the Puebla Conference. It has a continuing service of documentation and bibliography.

Centro Puebla (Aptdo. 80.978, Caracas 108, Venezuela).

Servir (Aptdo. 334, Jalapa, Ver., Mexico).

Revista Eclesiastica Brazileira (Editora Vozes, rua Frei Luis 100, Petropolis, RJ, Brazil).

Cross Currents, XXVIII, 1. (103 Van Houten Fields, West Nyack, N.Y. 10994).

IDOC-International, June-July 1978, editions in English and various other languages (Via Santa Maria dell'Anima 30, Roma 00186, Italy).

The Preliminary Document (PD) and the Working Document (WD) were prepared and issued in Spanish by the CELAM Secretariat (Aptdo. Aéreo 51086, Bogotá, Colombia).

The Final Document (preliminary) and the Final Document as amended in Rome before being made official by Pope John Paul have also been issued in Spanish by the CELAM secretariat. An English translation of the official text is available from the U.S. Catholic Conference (1312 Mass. Ave., N.W., Washington D.C. 20005).

Centro Antonio de Montesinos (Aptdo. Postal 19–377, Mexico 19, D.F.), *Puebla*, a continuing series of evaluations and commentaries on the F.D.

Books

Barnet, Richard and Muller, Ronald E. *Global Reach.* New York: Simon and Schuster, 1974.

Dussel, Enrique. *History and the Theology of Liberation.* Maryknoll, N.Y.: Orbis Books, 1976.

Gibellini, Rosino, ed. *Frontiers of Theology in Latin America.* Maryknoll, N.Y.: Orbis Books, 1979.

Gorostiaga, Xabier, ed. *Para Entender America Latina.* Panama: Centro de Estudios y Accion Social Panameño (Apartado 6–133, El Dorado, Panama), 1979.
Contributions of more than forty social scientists who worked as a team at Puebla and provided analyses and critiques to delegates and to the press, as the meeting proceeded. Coordinated by Richard Barnet, Luis A Gomez de Souza, Fernando Danel Janet and Xabier Gorostiaga, the group included Felipe Berryman, Frei Betto, Alfonso Castillo, Joe Collins, Enrique Dussel, Joseph Fitzpatrick, Isabel Letelier, Enrique Maza and Pedro Trigo.

Gremillion, Joseph. *The Gospel of Peace and Justice.* Maryknoll, N.Y.: Orbis Books, 1976.

Gutiérrez, Gustavo. *A Theology of Liberation.* Maryknoll, N.Y.: Orbis Books, 1973.

Hennelly, Alfred T. *Theologies in Conflict.* Maryknoll, N.Y.: Orbis Books, 1979.

Ledogar, Robert J. *Hungry for Profits.* New York: IDOC - North America, 1975.

MacEoin, Gary, ed. *Puebla: Moment of Decision for the Latin American Church.* A symposium in *Cross Currents,* Vol. XXVIII, No. 1, Spring 1978.

MacEoin, Gary. *Revolution Next Door: Latin America* in the 1970's. New York: Holt, Rinehart and Winston, 1971.

Moore Lappe, Frances and Collins, Joseph. *Food First.* Boston: Houghton Mifflin, 1977.

Segundo, Juan Luis. *Christology at the Crossroads: A Latin American Approach.* Maryknoll, N.Y.: Orbis Books, 1978.

Torres, Sergio and Eagleson, John, eds. *Theology* in *the Americas.* Maryknoll, N.Y.: Orbis Books, 1976.

Documentation

Between Honesty and Hope. Documents selected by the Committee for Social Action of the Peruvian Bishops. Maryknoll, N.Y.: Orbis Books, 1970.

Medellin Documents. Original Spanish published as *Documentos Finales de Medellin* (Buenos Aires: Ediciones Paulinas, 1969). English translation: *The Church in the Present-Day Transformation of Latin America in the Light of the Council* (Bogotá, Colombia, 1970).

The Church in Latin America from Medellin to Puebla. Rome: IDOC, 1978.

São Paulo: Growth and Poverty. A report from the São Paulo Justice and Peace Commission. English version—London: Bowerdean Press in association with the Catholic Institute for International Relations. (Obtainable from Justice and Peace, U.S. Catholic Conference, 1312 Mass. Ave., N.W., Wash. D.C. 20005).

Acknowledgments

We recognize with gratitude the general sharing of information by the worldwide staff of journalists, by theologians and social scientists, and by other members of the people of God of every ecclesiastical and social level from all parts of the hemisphere.

It was their faith, their hope, their commitment and their courage that inspired us to make this our contribution to the liberation of all who are oppressed and their oppressors.

Paul David Sholin, pastor of St. Mark's Presbyterian Church of Tucson shared our work and our life in Puebla. His understanding of Latin America is exceeded only by his desire to see the church totally committed to the reign of justice. We thank him for the profound insights he shared with us.

The many others whose contributions were particularly helpful include:

Jose Alvarez Icaza, Gary Campbell, and the CENCOS staff:

Hernan Leemrijse

Elizabeth M. Hollants

Enrique Maza

Gregory Bergman

Rosemary Ruether

Faith Annette Sand

Philip Berryman

Kathy Smalley

Paul Oullette

Bishop Leonidas Proano

Alfonso Castillo

Bernard Diederich

Luis del Valle

Peter Hinde

Marlene Tuininga

Julian Filakowski

Jim Andrews

Giancarlo Zizola and his colleagues
of the Italian press

Finally, we offer special thanks to those who have supported us at home, to Jo, Rita, Jim, Sean, Rob, and John C.

INDEX

Abbreviations

Puebla: Third Latin American Conference of Bishops
Medellin: Second L.A. Conference of Bishops
PD: Preliminary Document
WD: Working Document
FD: Final Document
RD: Revised Document
C de B: Communidades de base

133